EVERYTHING CHANGES

Also by Beverly Conyers:

Addict in the Family: Stories of Loss, Hope, and Recovery

EVERYTHING CHANGES

✦

Help for Families of Newly Recovering Addicts

Beverly Conyers

HAZELDEN®

Hazelden
Center City, Minnesota 55012
hazelden.org

Library of Congress Cataloging-in-Publication Data

Conyers, Beverly.
    Everything changes : help for families of newly recovering addicts / Beverly Conyers.
      p.   cm.
    Includes bibliographical references.
    ISBN 978-1-59285-697-8 (softcover)
     1. Alcoholics—Family relationships.   2. Drug addicts—Family relationships.
  3. Alcoholics—Rehabilitation.   4. Drug addicts—Rehabilitation.   I. Title.
    HV5123.C647 2009
    362.29'13—dc22

                                2008055459

Editor's note

The names, details, and circumstances may have been changed to protect the privacy of those mentioned in this publication.

This publication is not intended as a substitute for the advice of health care professionals.

Alcoholics Anonymous, AA, and the Big Book are registered trademarks of Alcoholics Anonymous World Services, Inc.

13 12 11 10   2 3 4 5 6

Cover design by Theresa Jaeger Gedig
Interior design by David Spohn
Typesetting by BookMobile Design and Publishing Services, Minneapolis, Minnesota

To Doris, whose wise and generous spirit was the inspiration for this book—and to travelers everywhere on the winding road to recovery

Contents

✦

PREFACE

In July 2000, I discovered that my twenty-three-year-old daughter—
a graceful blonde and the baby of the family—had become addicted
to heroin. Nothing could have prepared me for the devastation of
that moment, nor could I have anticipated the years of heartache
that lay ahead.

For many months, I was consumed by my daughter's addiction: What had caused it, what was it doing to her, and most of
all, how could I save her? I thought about her constantly; my
racing, terror-filled thoughts alternating with grief-inducing
memories of her as a little girl—twirling through the kitchen
in her ballet costume, opening a Christmas gift, hugging her
lop-eared dog.

I became obsessed with rescuing this child, with freeing her to
blossom into the lovely young woman she had promised to become. I was vigilant, persistent, making sure that she attended
counseling sessions and Twelve Step meetings, searching her face
and personal belongings (when I thought she wouldn't notice) for
signs of drug use. I learned everything I could from books, from
therapists, from other parents of addicted children—all with the
desperate determination to save my daughter.

In time, because we humans can't exist forever in a state of panic,
and because there are lessons to be learned even from the unthink-
able, I began to envision a book about addiction. I wanted to share
some of the knowledge I had gained and to offer the kind of support I had received from wonderful people whose wisdom and
kindness had lightened my darkest days. And I wanted to offer a

message of hope because, after all, hope sustains life, reminding us that anything is possible.

That book became *Addict in the Family: Stories of Loss, Hope, and Recovery*, published by Hazelden in August 2003. When I completed it, I thought I had said all I had to say about addiction. I had exhausted the topic and was ready to move on.

Several years later, I realized I was wrong.

My daughter has continued to struggle with addiction. There have been periods of sobriety and lapses into substance abuse. There have been sure signs of progress and long stretches of regression. I have begun to think of her as having one foot in recovery and the other in addiction. It is an unsettling state of affairs but not, I have learned, all that uncommon.

Recovery is hard. That may seem so obvious that it's hardly worth stating. Yet in our frustration with addiction and our desperation to see our loved ones turn their lives around, it is easy to overlook the simple fact: Recovery is hard. Addicted individuals have compromised their physical and mental health. They have damaged and lost significant relationships. Their self-esteem has suffered, and they face social stigmatization that impairs their ability to find jobs and housing. They often see themselves as outcasts, and too often society sees them that way as well.

The more I thought about the challenges my daughter and others like her face, the more I began to see the need for another book—one that focuses not on addiction itself but on its aftermath. What is the process of recovery? How do people change? And how can families and friends support their loved ones in this most daunting of endeavors?

With those questions in mind, I began to do research, to seek input from experts in the field, and to gather stories from people in recovery and their families. This book is the result of those efforts. My hope is that it will shed some light on the recovery process, and that it will be a source of comfort and guidance for anyone whose loved one is navigating the complex journey beyond addiction.

Beverly Conyers
November 2008

ACKNOWLEDGMENTS

I wish to thank the men and women who so generously shared their stories of recovery with me. I was repeatedly amazed and awed by your honesty, courage, and resilience. Thanks also to the family members who shared their tales of heartache and healing. You reminded me always of the power of patience and faith. I also wish to thank the men and women who allowed me a glimpse into the challenges and rewards of working with the addicted. I was inspired by your perseverance in the face of resistance and disappointment, and by your unwavering conviction that no one is beyond redemption. Thanks to Fran Bradshaw, LMHC; Patrice Muchowski, Sc.D.; J. David Mulrooney, LCSW, LADC-1; and Douglas Ziedonis, M.D., for your expert insight into the nature of addiction treatment. Thanks finally to my editor, Karen Chernyaev, who believed in this book from the start.

INTRODUCTION

Faith is the substance of things hoped for, the evidence of things not seen.
—HEBREWS 11:1

What is recovery? In a general sense, it is the restoration of health after an injury or illness. Because addiction is an illness of mind, body, and spirit, recovery from addiction implies holistic healing in which all facets of an individual's being evolve toward health.

To put it another way, recovery from addiction is a long-term journey of personal growth. It builds on abstinence from substances of abuse to encompass physical, emotional, social, and spiritual healing.

Recovery often begins with the acknowledgment that a problem exists. But like all ventures into the unknown territory of positive change, the journey is likely to be full of wrong turns and bumps in the road. It can sometimes resemble a maze more than a superhighway. To complicate matters, there is no single road to recovery.

For some addicted individuals, lasting recovery begins when they enter a good treatment facility, commit to individual counseling, or begin attending Twelve Step meetings. But this is not always the case. Slips and relapses are common. Many people enter multiple treatment programs over extended periods of time, only to resume their addictive behaviors after each attempt at sobriety.

Other individuals trace their recovery to "hitting bottom." Going to jail, losing a job, or simply being "sick and tired of being sick and tired" are all potential turning points into recovery. But "hitting bottom" is seldom a onetime event. Recidivism rates are high for people with addictions, and many people hit multiple "bottoms" before they are ready to commit to recovery.

Although events and circumstances can influence an individual's decision to change course, there is an internal factor that is of far more significance. That factor is readiness. People begin to recover from their addictions when they are ready to try to change their lives.

This is not to say that ambivalence disappears. We all feel a degree of doubt when we decide to change something in our lives, whether it's a job, a neighborhood, a relationship, or even a diet. The lure of the familiar is always powerful because it feels safe, even when it is destructive.

Despite the ambivalence that often accompanies early recovery, the journey can be said to begin when an addicted individual starts to make healthy choices. How long it will take and how successful that individual will be in reaching the desired destination—which for most people is some version of a stable, productive life—depend on many factors, including support.

Family and friends may be willing and eager to support their loved one's attempts at recovery. After all, they have witnessed firsthand the destructive course of addiction and, in the process, experienced wrenching heartache, fear, and despair. But what is their appropriate role in the process? What can they expect as their loved one begins to change? How can they maintain their own peace of mind? And how can they handle the inevitable bumps in the road?

This book is intended to serve as a resource for family and friends who are entering the uncharted territory of early recovery. Although the horizon beckons with tremendous promise, the immediate terrain is strewn with pitfalls. Confusion, uncertainty, and anxiety are common. Expectation and disappointment, relief and resentment, optimism and doubt all come together in a shifting tableau of emotional turmoil.

Despite the challenges, families who understand the inevitable ups and downs of early recovery put themselves in a strong position to offer their loved one meaningful support. Equally important, they are better able to maintain their own peace of mind as the path to recovery unfolds—and everything changes.

Chapter 1

THE JOURNEY BEGINS

A journey of a thousand miles begins with a single step.
—Lao Tzu

The young woman at the front of the room is small, just over five feet tall, with a thin, childlike body and pale oval face. She wears faded jeans, sneakers, and a baggy sweater with arms that hang almost to her fingertips. Her long, straight hair is dyed a bold shade of red.

She pushes a strand of hair off her forehead and gazes at a point somewhere beyond the audience. When she speaks, her voice is like a whisper. "I'm Maggie, and I'm an addict and an alcoholic."

Thirty or so people sit before her in the church basement meeting hall. Most of them seem patient, attentive, and respectful, even though they are about to hear a story they have heard many times before. Not from Maggie, necessarily, but from others like her—especially themselves. Even though the story is an old one, it is new and painful each time it's told.

"I started drinking when I was thirteen," she confides with a tremor in her voice. "My friend's brother would buy us beer and pot. The only time I felt good was when I was stoned. Then I started doing acid." By the time she was fifteen, she was getting high four or five times a week, and within a year she was snorting cocaine, OxyContin, heroin—just about anything she could get her hands on. She dropped out of school, lost a series of waitressing jobs, and wound up working the streets.

Now twenty-four, Maggie has been in jail three times and tried rehab eight or nine times. "I got out of rehab two weeks ago" she says. "I've been clean and sober three months and fourteen days."

There is a brief burst of applause, bringing a sweet, timid smile to Maggie's face. She draws a deep breath and tells the group, "I got my three-month coin and now I'm working on my six-month one. I'm gonna do it this time."

Flushed and proud, she returns to her seat amid whispers of encouragement. It is a happy moment for Maggie, one filled with hope and vague visions of a better life. But already she can feel the tremors of self-doubt. She has been clean many times before—once for five whole months—but she always returned to the old ways.

Can things really be different this time?

Across town, Maggie's mother is wondering the same thing. She washes the supper dishes that Maggie didn't have time to help her with and prays that her daughter is actually at the AA meeting she claimed to be going to.

Maggie has been a source of sorrow and worry for so long that her mother has a hard time remembering when it was otherwise. Once an affectionate, happy child, Maggie grew into an anxious, secretive young woman with erratic mood swings and evasive silences. Time and again, Maggie showed herself to be unreliable, deceitful, and thoughtless. She dropped out of college, distanced herself from her family, and—on the rare occasions when she showed up for a birthday or holiday gathering—was not above helping herself to ten or twenty dollars from her mother's purse.

In time, her mother learned that what she had attributed to a psychological disorder—maybe severe depression or anxiety—was in fact addiction. The knowledge was shocking and at the same time so glaringly obvious that she still wonders how she could have been so blind for so long.

Maggie has been living at home for about two weeks, since finishing her latest stint in rehab. During that time, her moods have been up and down—hopeful and optimistic one moment, withdrawn and irritable the next. Her mother has tried to maintain a sense of balance, to not expect too much. She has learned from bitter experience that completing rehab doesn't guarantee anything. She knows that she has no more control over Maggie's recovery than she does over her addiction.

Still, she can't help but nurture a little kernel of hope. What if this really is the time that Maggie's recovery begins in earnest? What if the years of heartache are finally coming to an end? What if the miracle she has heard about in other people's lives is about to transform her own? And if Maggie is ready to begin changing her life, what can her mother do to help?

Questions like these are common when our loved one takes those early, tentative steps toward recovery from addiction. It's a confusing time in which we alternate between hope and fear and when our loved one's moods may swing unpredictably from one day to the next. We both hope that everything will get better, yet the possibility of relapse lurks in our minds. We long for normalcy, yet there is no going back to the way things were before addiction came into our lives. Some of us may be even unhappier during early recovery than we were during active addiction—for a while. That is because early recovery is a time of emotional turmoil.

Our loved one is learning to function without substances and redefining his sense of identity. We are learning to find new ways of viewing our relationship and ourselves. Together we are challenged to learn new attitudes and behaviors and to reexamine long-held assumptions about each other.

If all of this sounds difficult, it is. Change of this magnitude does not come easily. But early recovery is also a time of great promise. The path to a richer, more rewarding life lies before us. By knowing what to expect and gaining a deeper understanding of the struggle for recovery, we will be better able to appreciate the journey and handle the inevitable ups and downs along the way.

THE FAMILY'S ROLE IN EARLY RECOVERY

Therapists say that addiction is a family disease: When one member of the family is ill, the entire group is affected. Those of us who have lived with active addiction know this to be true. Many of us have joined our loved one in the game of denial, pretending that nothing is wrong or that things aren't as bad as they appear to be. Many of us have neglected our own needs and interests in an effort not to "upset" our loved one and thus set off another bout of drinking or drugging. Many of us have become consummate "rescuers," always ready to offer solutions and save our loved one from facing the serious negative consequences of addiction.

As unhealthy as all of this sounds, it is at first natural. We want to help the person who is sick and suffering. We are afraid that if we do nothing, our loved one will die—if not the immediate, brutal death of an overdose or accident, then the slow, painful decay of body, mind, and spirit. As one father put it, "Watching my son killing himself is the hardest thing I've ever been through. It's like a part of me is dying too."

In our anxiety, what started as a natural desire to help turns into a series of unhealthy responses. We are apt to focus all our thoughts, emotions, and energy on our addicted loved one for a very long time. We begin to view the world, ourselves, and others through the distorted lens of addiction. We question our own sense of reality, second-guess ourselves about the "right" thing to do, and replay the past over and over in our minds in our attempts to understand the incomprehensible.

In time, our obsession with the addict affects other members of the family, either drawing them into our own emotional turmoil or arousing feelings of neglect, resentment, or anger. Addiction permeates our lives, becoming in a very real sense a family disease. Most of us take a long time to fully grasp the harsh realities of addiction and an even longer time to develop the necessary coping skills for keeping our own lives somewhat sane and manageable.

The bedrock lessons of coping with addiction—that we cannot enable and that we must detach from our loved one's problems—come to most of us only after a long and painful struggle.

But what about recovery? How does a loved one's recovery affect a family, and to what extent (if any) should family members become involved in the effort to get clean?

As with everything about addiction, there are no easy answers. Family support is frequently cited as an important factor in successful recovery from addiction. Knowing that someone believes in you and is rooting for you can be a powerful source of strength when the inevitable challenges of recovery arise. But understanding the value of offering support and knowing how much and what kind of support to give can be two very different things.

One young woman in long-term recovery stated, "Every time I was in detox, my mother would be there for me. She was always there with words of encouragement. She's a big part of the reason I got clean."

On the other hand, a young man expressed the opposite point of view when he said, "My mother was always hovering over me when I went into treatment. I was so afraid of letting her down that I couldn't deal with it. It was too much pressure."

One counselor addressed the family's dilemma with this advice: "When the addiction is active, families should step away. When recovery is under way, they should move closer. However, sometimes families need to give their loved one space. It can take time before the addict is ready to reengage with the family. And families may need to take a wait-and-see approach before they're able to offer support."

To shed some light on how to best help ourselves, our family, and our recovering loved one through early recovery, it is helpful to take a look at addiction and how it's treated.

THE ADDICTED BRAIN

Addiction is a disease that causes profound, long-lasting changes in the way the brain functions. It begins with repeated exposure to chemicals that stimulate sensations of pleasure or inhibit perception of pain. In time, the brain's complex processes responsible for observation, reasoning, emotions, and self-preservation become distorted. A dangerous reality takes hold, in which the addicted brain functions primarily to obtain increasing amounts of pleasure-producing, pain-inhibiting substances.

It is worth noting that even compulsive and addictive behaviors that don't involve drugs or alcohol—gambling, sex, shopping, and eating disorders, for example—can stimulate the brain's production of dopamine, endorphins, and other chemicals to produce a natural "high," thus rewarding and reinforcing the addictive behavior.

In the early stages, most addicted individuals believe they have control over their use of substances—that they can choose how much and how often they will use and that they can stop whenever they want to. They eventually learn otherwise.

The chemical and physical changes produced by repeated use of alcohol and other drugs derail connectors within the brain, disrupting the flow of information in bizarre and unnatural ways. The distinction between fantasy and reality, between self-preservation and self-destruction, becomes blurred. Emotional connections to family and friends wither away. And the perception of action and consequence is distilled into one compelling, overarching idea: The presence of chemicals brings pleasure (or at least relief from pain), and their absence produces pain.

The addicted brain creates its own reality, and what began as a choice becomes a powerful compulsion to obtain and use chemicals even in the face of serious negative consequences.

Erik, a twenty-eight-year-old man whose weekend drinking binges in high school morphed into an addiction to cocaine, thought he had his drug use under control. "I was working in an auto body shop, and for a few years everything was great," he said. "I'd do my partying on the weekends but I wouldn't go near the stuff during the week. Just like high school. But then the weekends started running into Mondays and Tuesdays, and all my money was going to coke. I couldn't stop myself."

Erik's freefall continued until he was arrested for driving under the influence at the age of twenty-six. He was put on probation and subjected to random drug tests. His fiancée threatened to leave him if he didn't get help. "I got into treatment and really worked the program," he said. "I've been clean almost two years now."

The program imposed a strict regimen of counseling and group meetings. "They were good. They made me toe the line," he admits. "But I could've walked any time I wanted to. A lot of guys did. For some reason, I didn't want to. I wanted to make it work."

Erik's desire to get clean played an important role in his recovery. Attitude and commitment are key components of any successful endeavor. But few people achieve anything of significance—and being in recovery from addiction *is* a significant achievement—without help from others along the way. For Erik, as for many people struggling with addiction, help first came in the form of an effective treatment program.

TWO MYTHS ABOUT TREATMENT

The role of treatment in addressing substance abuse is easily misunderstood. On one hand, desperate families turn to treatment with expectations of an immediate cure. On the other hand, because recovery can take so long and relapse is so prevalent, they sometimes conclude that treatment doesn't work. Neither view takes into account the complex physiological and psychological aspects of addiction, and neither one is accurate.

In the early stages of coping with addiction, family expectations about treatment tend to run high. I remember taking my twenty-three-year-old daughter to an outpatient program after discovering that she was addicted to heroin. We both signed up for counseling—I signed up to learn how to help her, and she signed up to learn how to stay off drugs. In my naiveté, my expectations weren't all that different from what they might have been if she'd had a cavity and I was taking her to the dentist. She had a problem and here were the professionals who were going to fix it.

My attitude was typical. As one therapist put it, "I know that families want me to do an 'addictectomy' on their loved one. They want me to reach in there and permanently remove the addiction. I tell them that I wish I could but it's just not possible. Recovery can be a long process, and there's no such thing as one treatment fits all."

Popular culture adds to the perception that treatment in itself can solve the problem of addiction. Magazines and tabloids are filled with stories of substance-abusing celebrities who enter rehab and emerge one or two months later, "cured" and ready to resume a more responsible lifestyle. Television programs regularly feature "ordinary people" whose lives were destroyed by addiction, only to be rescued by an intervention and admittance to a treatment facility. The message is that once an addicted individual enters treatment, the worst is over and life is good again.

The reality is usually quite different. Although some people leave treatment and never touch a drink or drug again, many others start using again and eventually return to rehab one or more times. This has led some people to conclude that treatment does not work. In fact, success rates for substance abuse treatment are similar to those for diabetes, asthma, and other chronic, recurring illnesses.

In *Principles of Drug Addiction Treatment,* the National Institute on Drug Abuse explains it this way:

> In spite of scientific evidence that establishes the effectiveness of drug abuse treatment, many people believe that treatment is ineffective. In part, this is because of unrealistic expectations. Many people equate addiction with simply using drugs and therefore expect that addiction should be cured quickly, and if it is not, treatment is a failure. In reality, because addiction is a chronic disorder, the ultimate goal of long-term abstinence often requires sustained and repeated treatment episodes.[1]

In other words, treatment works, but some patients may need multiple treatment experiences before recovery is stabilized. The effects of treatment are cumulative, and with every treatment episode and relapse, patients learn something about themselves and their addiction. What was gained in treatment is not lost—even though it may be put on the back burner for a while.

In many ways, addiction is no different from other chronic conditions—including eating disorders, mental illnesses, and a host of physical maladies—that require repeated treatment episodes over lengthy periods of time. If we consider the problem of obesity, for example, we begin to understand the complexity of treating addiction.

A MULTILAYERED CHALLENGE

Americans spend an estimated $46 billion a year on diet products, programs, and self-help books, hoping to lose weight and improve their health. Yet the number of obese Americans has roughly doubled since the 1970s. Today, approximately 60 percent of adults are overweight, and about half of those are clinically obese. Complicating the picture even more, two-thirds of

American dieters regain all the weight they have lost within a year, and 97 percent gain it back within five years.

What's going on?

Many factors make weight loss difficult, including the fact that changing our habits is hard—particularly habits that are linked to the brain's natural reward system. When an action or substance makes us feel good, we want more of it, even in the face of negative consequences.

This biological reality is complicated further in the case of chemical addiction. Physical changes have taken place in the brain. Irrational thoughts have become ingrained. Dysfunctional behaviors have taken root. The individual's ability to function at work, with family, and in the broader community have become significantly impaired. And the addict's value system has become so distorted that substances have become the only absolute good.

Is it any wonder, then, that treating addiction is so very challenging? Effective treatment goes far beyond the cleansing of addictive chemicals from the body. It addresses multiple aspects of an addict's life, seeking to promote physical, psychological, social, and spiritual healing.

Lynne, a first-grade teacher and the mother of three grown sons, has come to understand the challenges of addiction treatment. Her middle child, Ben, has been in sixteen treatment programs—some for only a day or two—over the past two years. In her darkest hours, she wonders if he will ever be able to function on his own.

"He was kind of a wild kid," she recalls. "We caught him smoking cigarettes in the garage when he was eleven, and the next year he was caught shoplifting at a convenience store. But we did some family counseling, and the kid he'd been hanging around with moved away, and after that he settled down."

Ben worked in a pizza shop in high school and found a job as an apprentice carpenter after graduation. He rented an apartment with some friends, paid his bills, and had a couple of nice girl-friends that Lynne says "he came close to marrying." But some-where along the line he picked up drug and alcohol problems. He started having anger issues, leading one of his girlfriends to take out a restraining order against him. He got in a series of car ac-cidents, lost his job, and moved back in with his family.

"We told him he had to go to this outpatient program that's supposed to be good," Lynne says. "So far, he's doing it, but we're holding our breath."

A NEW BEGINNING

Ben's story is all too common. My own daughter had a "wild streak" as a child, but after high school she moved in with her boyfriend and worked steadily as a nurse's aide. She paid her bills, kept her apartment clean, and talked about applying to nursing school. I was relieved to see that she was "growing up."

Then, her boyfriend moved out and her life seemed to fall apart. Although it would take many months before I broke through my own denial and confronted the fact that she was addicted to heroin, I was horrified by the changes I saw in her. She lost her job. Her apartment became filthy. Her clothes were sweat-stained and dotted with tiny burn holes. She stopped talking of going to nursing school or of changing her life at all.

Eventually, she agreed to enter an outpatient treatment pro-gram. I spent a lot of time waiting for treatment to "kick in." She attended her counseling sessions faithfully—for a while—and went to Twelve Step meetings, but she still seemed adrift on the fringes of society. She still seemed incapable of managing her life. I grew impatient. Was treatment not the answer after all? Why was it taking so long? Why couldn't someone make her change?

Looking back, I realize that, like many family members, I had little understanding of the complexities of addiction. I tended to think that if she stopped using heroin, her life would get better.

And there is some basis for my belief. The bedrock of recovery is abstinence from addictive, mood-altering chemicals. But it is also true that for sobriety to be achieved and maintained, our loved one needs to work through multiple layers of dysfunctional thoughts and behaviors. She must replace unhealthy attitudes and belief systems with new ways of thinking and understanding. And she must acquire new skills for long-term management of a chronic disease.

It was only after I began to understand the enormity of the physical, psychological, and social challenges presented by addiction that I began to adopt more realistic expectations of treatment. I learned that treatment, although a significant step in the recovery process, is not an end in itself. It is a beginning.

THREE TREATMENT GOALS

Treatment is generally acknowledged to play a significant role in promoting recovery from addiction to alcohol and other drugs. But not all treatment programs are equally effective, and not all programs are suitable for every addicted individual. To better understand how treatment contributes to the recovery process, it is worth examining trends in substance abuse treatment today.

Most treatment centers now use some combination of motivational enhancement therapy (MET), cognitive-behavioral therapy (CBT), and the Twelve Step principles of Alcoholics Anonymous (AA). MET is a patient-centered approach that enlists addicts in identifying and setting their own therapeutic goals, starting with where they are at in accepting their addiction. CBT helps addicts replace delusional addiction thinking with healthier reality-based thinking that promotes positive behaviors. The Twelve Steps give patients a framework for ongoing recovery in self-help programs in their community (such as AA or NA). The aim is to change unhealthy behaviors and self-defeating emotions within a framework that promotes abstinence from substances of abuse.

Increasingly, effective treatment programs focus on three fundamental goals:

1. *Promoting abstinence.* Addiction is a chronic illness that feeds on drugs. Only by abstaining from addictive, mood-altering chemicals can a person begin to recover.

2. *Improving mental and physical health.* Many addicted individuals have co-occurring mental and physical health problems. If these problems are not adequately treated, the likelihood of recovery from substance abuse is greatly diminished.

3. *Facilitating the development of skills for a drug-free lifestyle.* Managing the tasks of day-to-day living—including self-care, household and money management, working, and maintaining rewarding relationships—is a fundamental element of sustained recovery.

Although programs vary in the amount of attention they give to each of these goals, research has shown that when treatment addresses all three areas, clients are more likely to achieve and sustain a meaningful recovery.

ADDICTION TREATMENT TODAY

The quality of treatment programs varies widely. Furthermore, even the best program can be right for one patient and not entirely appropriate for another. There is no such thing as one program fits all, and addicts may need to try a number of different programs before they find one that works for them. Broadly speaking, treatment is available in three different settings: inpatient, outpatient, and extended care.

Inpatient Treatment

Many inpatient facilities have medical units equipped to safely handle detoxification, the initial and sometimes dangerous phase of care in which addictive chemicals are cleansed from the body. Some treatment facilities partner with a hospital to handle this phase. Detoxification is a first step in recovery and does not, in itself, do anything to address addiction. It should not be confused with treatment.

Inpatient treatment generally lasts from seven to twenty-eight days, although some facilities offer programs lasting six months or longer. Settings vary widely, from hospitals to upscale retreats to criminal justice facilities. During treatment, patients are completely immersed in recovery. They learn that they have a chronic disease that will require lifelong management. They learn about the physical and psychological impact of addiction and begin to develop tools for maintaining abstinence. Through participation in group and individual counseling sessions, they also begin to examine their beliefs and emotions and discover new ways of responding to the world. Therapeutic sessions help patients gain self-awareness and build motivation for continuing their recovery.

The advantage of inpatient treatment is that it allows patients to focus solely on getting better, without the stress or distraction of everyday life. The disadvantage is that it requires them to take time away from home and work, which may present a hardship for themselves and their families.

Outpatient Treatment

There are significant differences among outpatient programs. Some are designed primarily to educate participants about the effects of alcohol and other drugs. Intensive outpatient programs, on the other hand, are similar in scope to inpatient treatment. They combine education about the disease of addiction along with group counseling and individual therapy. They focus on helping patients develop the skills and motivation necessary for sustaining sobriety. Most intensive outpatient programs require patients to attend sessions several hours a day, five days a week, for over a period of a month or more.

In some ways, outpatient treatment is more challenging than inpatient treatment because patients must try to maintain sobriety while continuing to function in their daily lives. However, the advantage of outpatient treatment is that it allows patients to continue to fulfill their family and employment obligations while getting help.

A Note about Methadone Maintenance

Some outpatient programs offer medically assisted treatment for opiate and alcohol addictions. For example, methadone has been used for more than forty years to treat opiate addiction and has been proven effective in preventing opiate withdrawal, blocking the high produced by opiate use and decreasing opiate cravings. Being stabilized on methadone has been shown to reduce risky behaviors associated with HIV infection and criminal activity. Some patients remain in methadone maintenance treatment for many years in order to prevent relapse to opiate use.

However, methadone and other addiction medications will not in and of themselves promote recovery. To help patients attain a stable, productive life, well-run medically assisted treatment programs include education, individual and group therapy, and access to needed medical, psychological, and social services.

Extended Care

Extended programs—sometimes up to a year or more—are posttreatment facilities designed to help patients reenter society while living in a highly supportive environment. Halfway houses, a common type of extended care program, encourage residents to work, develop social networks, and build day-to-day living skills. Most have on-site Twelve Step meetings as well as house managers who monitor the progress of residents' recovery.

OTHER ROADS TO RECOVERY

Not everyone who goes through treatment finds recovery, and not everyone in recovery has gone through treatment. Some people quit cold turkey and never touch a drink or drug again. And numerous people have found recovery solely through the Twelve Steps of AA, founded in the 1930s by two alcoholics, Bill Wilson and Dr. Bob Smith. Both men managed to overcome their addictions through a process of (1) accepting their power- lessness over alcohol (or other drugs), (2) surrendering to a Power greater than themselves for help, (3) doing a thorough moral inventory and personal housecleaning, including making amends to the people they harmed, (4) being of service to other alcoholics and addicts, and (5) attending Twelve Step mutual support groups.

Wilson described their approach to recovery in a book he called *Alcoholics Anonymous.* In it, he spelled out twelve steps alco- holics could take to achieve personal growth and free themselves from the bonds of addiction. Those steps still form the philo- sophical core of AA and its many offshoots, including Narcotics Anonymous and—for families of substance abusers—Al-Anon and Nar-Anon.

Today, millions of people worldwide participate in Twelve Step programs, a testament to the effectiveness of the approach.

The basic tenets of Twelve Step programs are deceptively simple, but they contain the timeless wisdom found in most of the world's great spiritual philosophies, promoting humility, honesty, and service. Following the Steps allows program mem- bers to create more satisfying lives within a belief system that promotes healing from shame and isolation—two damaging con- sequences of addiction—along with gentle guidance for rebuild- ing their lives "one day at a time."

Twelve Step programs are not for everyone—just as no formal treatment program is right for everyone. But there is no denying that the Twelve Steps have made a profound and lasting impact on our understanding of addiction, and that they have lighted the way for millions on the path to recovery.

WHOSE RECOVERY IS IT?

Most families are unsure of what to expect when their loved one completes a formal treatment program. They may hope for a completely changed person, someone whose character defects have been magically "cured" and whose substance abuse issues have been left behind.

In reality, treatment programs are a starting point. They give patients the tools to maintain sobriety, but it is up to the patient to use those tools over the long, hard road of recovery that lies ahead. Another way of looking at it is that, like all of us, addicts in early recovery are a work in progress. There is still much emotional and social healing to be done.

When Mitchell's wife came home after completing a four-month court-ordered residential treatment program for alcohol addiction, he was vigilant about supervising her budding recovery. "I watched her like a hawk," he admits. "I wanted to know what she was thinking and feeling every minute. If she was down, I started to feel panicky. If she was in a good mood, I got suspicious."

Mitchell drove her to counseling sessions and AA meetings. He bought books for her to read and cut out helpful articles from newspapers and magazines. He made sure that she ate healthy meals and that she went to bed at a "reasonable" hour, even if she insisted that she wasn't tired. "I told the kids that Mommy was sick and needed peace and quiet so she could get better," he recalls.

This state of affairs lasted about two months, until she got her license back and began driving herself where she needed to go. She told her husband to stop trying to control her. "Then I got pissed," Mitchell says. "After everything I'd been through and everything I'd done for her, she couldn't wait to get away from me. At least that's how I took it. I thought we were in this together. It took me a long time to accept she had to do it without me."

Mitchell's story is not uncommon. For family members who desperately want their loved one to get clean, finding the line between being supportive and being controlling can be an ongoing challenge. Addiction has caused us repeated heartache and disappointment. It has robbed us of our dreams of how life should be. It has put our loved one's life at risk and strained relationships within the entire family.

Of course we want recovery to happen! And we are afraid that if we don't do our part, it will slip away.

It is at just this moment—when the path to recovery seems so very precarious—that it is helpful to step back and get a better perspective of the situation. The reality is, we don't have the power to control another person's recovery. We just don't.

We can offer encouragement and support. We can try to establish a positive environment. We can help our loved one access needed services. But we cannot make recovery happen. That task belongs to the addict, and we muddy the situation if we assume our loved one's challenges as our own.

M. Scott Peck, author of *The Road Less Traveled,* wrote that "A major characteristic of genuine love is that the distinction between oneself and the other is always maintained and preserved." He is talking about the need to set boundaries, to have our own identities that are not merged with another, no matter how badly we long for that person's happiness.

When we step in and take on responsibilities that are not our own, we weaken the people we love. We send the message that we don't believe they're smart enough or good enough to make it without us. We also set ourselves up for a big fall if things don't work out the way we'd planned. Resentment on both sides is the end result of trying to control someone else.

The solution is to allow our loved ones to manage their own recovery. As one therapist put it, "Families sometimes have a hard time with early recovery because it's a time of uncertainty. Things don't always go smoothly. But they need to accept the fact that they can't control the situation. Families can give encouragement and support, but they can't be responsible for their loved one's recovery."

FACING OUR OWN FEARS AND EXPECTATIONS

Recovery—like addiction—doesn't happen in a vacuum. Not surprisingly, we may find ourselves grappling with conflicting emotions when recovery begins. One moment we may find ourselves hoping for a perfect ending, and in the next moment we find ourselves fearing that it is too good to be true.

The emotional roller coaster that characterizes early recovery for the addict pulls the family along as well.

There is no denying that the years of active addiction have taken their toll. Some of us were robbed and cheated by our addicted loved one. Some of us were emotionally or physically abused. All of us were lied to.

When the addict begins to get better, the hurt, anxiety, and frustration don't just go away. We can't suddenly change our feelings. Our ability to offer support may be limited by our own desire to protect ourselves from further pain.

That is not a bad thing.

Hope—a longtime member of Al-Anon—recalled that when her adult daughter came home to live after being in jail and then a halfway house, "We took it on a month-by-month basis. I said we'd see how it went, and if it didn't work out, she'd have to find someplace else to live. I was afraid to trust her."

As much as she loved her daughter, Hope was cautious. "This disease is tricky," she explained. "You can see what you want to see."

As months went by and her daughter proved herself to be reliable and honest, Hope's trust began to grow. "She'd see me doing the dishes and she'd say, 'Let me do that. You sit down.' She came home from her meetings exactly when she said she would, or she'd call if she was going to be late and ask if that was all right," Hope said. "She had changed, but I hadn't yet. It took a while."

Hope's initial caution was a reasonable response to her daughter's homecoming. She was willing to offer support, but she was not willing to put up with the negative behaviors that go along with active addiction. She had established limits, and by doing so, taken steps to protect her own well-being.

Addiction teaches us many lessons. One of the most profound is that we cannot control anyone except ourselves. The lesson applies equally to recovery.

The recovery of a loved one is sure to arouse our hopes and fears, expectations and uncertainty. But we do not have to be buffeted by the inevitable ups and downs of the recovery process. By remembering to take care of ourselves, the journey can be one of growth and discovery—for us as well as for our loved one.

TIPS FOR DEALING WITH EARLY RECOVERY

Supporting the Addict

1. Get educated about addiction. The better you understand the disease, the more realistic you can be in your expectations and the more effective you can be in your efforts to support recovery.

2. Accept that maintaining sobriety is the addict's number one priority. Other goals and responsibilities will be addressed in time, but for the first year or so, the addict's primary focus should be on staying clean.

3. Don't have alcohol or other substances of abuse in the house. Don't drink in front of the addict in early recovery. Alcohol and other drugs permeate our society. In time, the addict must learn to maintain sobriety even when exposed to chemicals of abuse. But in the early months, avoid exposing your loved one to temptation.

4. Don't try to manage the recovery. Things may not appear to be progressing as fast as you would like. You may wish

that your loved one had a different sponsor or a better counselor. You may believe that a different AA meeting would be more helpful. Let your loved one decide.

5. Accept that the journey may be long and bumpy. Personal growth is a lifelong process with ups and downs. Recovery, a form of personal growth, takes a long time.

Supporting Yourself

1. Make your own well-being your top priority. Taking care of yourself helps insulate you from the inevitable ups and downs of recovery. With everything you do, think *extreme self-care.*

2. Seek out a mutual support group such as Al-Anon or Nar-Anon. Sharing worries and concerns—as well as successes!—with people who have been there relieves us of some of our burdens and helps us remember to keep the focus on ourselves.

3. Establish limits. Decide what is acceptable in terms of how you want to be treated. Make your limits clear to your loved one.

4. Cultivate hope. Active addiction can lead us into a habitual attitude of fear and pessimism. Yet an attitude is just a mind-set, not a reality. Work to replace negative attitudes with hope. A hopeful environment promotes recovery for both your loved one and yourself.

5. Avoid unrealistic expectations. Don't look for perfection and don't expect too much too soon. The person in early recovery is the same person as before, and is only beginning the long process of change.

CHAPTER 2

>←

THE HARD REALITIES
OF EARLY RECOVERY

Not everything that is faced can be changed,
but nothing can be changed until it is faced.
—JAMES BALDWIN

"I didn't know it was going to be so hard," the woman seated next to me says. She is a plump and pretty young mother with curly black hair and a round, flushed face. Today her voice is throaty with choked-back tears.

There are five of us in the circle, not including the therapist—all of us parents or spouses of people with addictions. As usual, we have been asked to give an account of how our week has gone.

"I mean, he's been sober six months now," she continues. "He does his meetings and everything, but I know he's struggling. He's been so moody. Any time I try to bring up something important, he shuts me out. I can't talk about the bills or things around the house that need to be fixed. He'll just walk away."

We nod sympathetically while she wipes her eyes with a tissue.

"I can tell you, I'm in that house with him and three kids, and it can get real lonely sometimes. Real lonely."

The therapist, a kindly man in his mid-forties, speaks up. "It doesn't sound like he's able to give you the kind of support you need right now. It sounds like he still has a lot of growing to do."

She nods her head. "He hasn't had a drink. That's one good thing. But I'm so scared he will."

There's a murmur of understanding. We have all had the good fortune of seeing our loved ones move from active addiction into recovery. Some of them are newly sober, and others have been clean more than a year. But instead of the relief we had expected to feel, most of us in our little support group are experiencing a whole host of uneasy emotions—in part because the reality of early recovery hasn't matched our expectations.

As many therapists remind us, sobriety is only the first step in recovery. It can be a tough slog from getting sober to getting better. Our loved one is learning new ways of living and being, and we're adjusting to his newfound sobriety.

What he says makes sense. But it doesn't completely erase the anxiety we're feeling. We've wanted so badly for recovery to happen. Now that it has, how much longer must we wait for things to really improve?

THE PHYSICAL BASIS OF ADDICTION

One of the most surprising—and disappointing—discoveries about early recovery is that things don't seem to change all that much. Not at first. The use of substances has stopped. The unexplained absences may have stopped. But the irritability and mood swings may be as bad as ever—maybe worse. And life's fundamental issues are still to be dealt with.

As my therapist put it, sobriety doesn't solve problems. It simply makes it possible for problems to be solved.

To better understand why sobriety is simply the first step in the journey, it is worth reviewing what is known about how addiction affects the brain.

For many years, alcoholism and other addictions were widely regarded as evidence of moral weakness and lack of willpower. It was believed that addiction was a choice, and the inexplicable choice of self-destructive behavior was a sign not of sickness but of a deeply flawed character. As addiction so often leads to irresponsible and even antisocial conduct, the condition became further stigmatized. People with addictions were viewed as not only weak and immoral, they were seen as fundamentally "bad."

Society's attitudes are slowly changing, but the stigma of addiction has been powerful and persistent. To this day, individuals in recovery from addiction may find themselves shut out from job and housing opportunities. They may face rejection in social settings. Their families may suffer the isolating effects of shame and embarrassment at having an addict in the family.

All this occurs more than forty years after the American Medical Association and American Psychiatric Association first defined alcoholism—and by extension other chemical addictions—as a disease!

The problem is that addiction does not, on the face of it, fit our conventional understanding of diseases. After all, addiction begins with the voluntary act of consuming an addictive substance and worsens with the voluntary act of continued use. An element of choice is always present, no matter how entrenched the addiction.

Nevertheless, many diseases, including heart disease, lung cancer, and emphysema, can result from voluntary exposure to a chemical—in this case, nicotine. Because it is clear that nicotine damages the body's respiratory and cardiovascular systems, we readily accept that it can cause diseases. What we don't see is that nicotine and other addictive substances also damage the way the brain's circuitry functions. All chemicals of abuse cause changes within the brain that distort perception and reinforce addiction.

Addiction has been shown to have a genetic component comparable to that seen in other chronic diseases. Studies suggest that only about one in ten people who try an addictive substance will ultimately get hooked. For those who do, initial encounters with substances are overwhelmingly compelling. Many addicted individuals describe the high from their very first drink as being more wonderful than falling in love—the thing they have been looking for all their lives. It is as if the foreign substance has triggered something in their brains that was there all along, waiting for the right chemical cue.

In our drug-saturated society, it is all too likely that the right chemical cue will present itself—often to adolescents, who are vulnerable to suggestion and who tend to see themselves as invincible.

Getting Hooked

Addicts are notorious for their resistance to treatment. Time and again they will reject or abandon the path to healing and instead embrace the very substances that perpetuate their illness.

That is, at least in part, because substances of abuse cause profound changes deep within the brain. What can look to observers like a stubborn or even willfully perverse course of action may be, in fact, the result of an impaired ability to process information. While it is true that individual responsibility cannot be discounted when considering the disease of addiction—it is individual responsibility, after all, that offers the possibility of recovery—it is equally true that addiction damages the brain's chemical and electrical circuitry to the point where it affects decision making.

Our brains contain a natural reward system—the production of pleasurable sensations in response to certain experiences. This mechanism is designed to promote activities that ensure our survival as a species. Both food and sex, for example, can produce intense feelings of pleasure. The complex process behind those good feelings is dramatically altered by substances of abuse.

Within the brain are billions of nerve cells (neurons) that communicate with each other via electrical impulses carried by chemical messengers (neurotransmitters) in a kind of perpetual chain reaction. Each neurotransmitter is specialized to deliver specific messages related to anything from motor activity to memory to pleasure and pain.

Several neurotransmitters play key roles within the reward system, but the one most targeted by substances of abuse is dopamine, the pleasure messenger. Alcohol, amphetamines, cocaine, nicotine, and opiates—the five substances considered the most difficult to give up—all flood the brain with dopamine, although their mechanism for doing so differs.

Regardless of the mechanics, the end result of a rush of dopamine is a sensation of intense pleasure. A recovering heroin addict who had been clean seven years remembered the heroin high as "the most wonderful feeling in the world." A recovering crack addict recalled that one hit of the drug made him feel "like I was king of the world. I was untouchable." A recovering alcoholic said, "Life was beautiful and I loved everyone, for a while, anyway."

Addictive substances bypass the normal routes to satisfaction—food, sex, friendships, accomplishment, and so on—and deliver a dose of pleasure far more potent than those produced by ordinary means. One dose of cocaine, for example, can release up to ten times the amount of dopamine produced by a good meal. But a continual assault on the brain's reward system is not without consequences.

Coming Down

Nature, including the human brain, always strives to strike a balance. So as chemicals cause abnormal amounts of dopamine to flood the reward system, the brain attempts to adjust by depleting excess dopamine. As dopamine levels decline, so does the ability to experience pleasure. As a result, a dose that used to deliver a high can no longer do so and greater amounts of the addictive substance must be used. Tolerance develops and the good feelings produced by the substance become more elusive.

Even worse, the brain's reward system is short-circuited. It no longer produces dopamine in response to such ordinary cues as food, sex, and relationships. It stops making dopamine because it no longer needs to. The drug is doing the brain's job. The addictive substance becomes the brain's *only* source of pleasure, to the exclusion of everything and everyone else.

In time, addicted individuals use chemicals not so much to feel good as to feel "normal." And when the addictive substance is withheld, intense distress sets in.

The addicted brain, which has learned to equate chemicals with survival, generates a cacophony of alarm signals in its clamor for relief. The result—withdrawal—is the unavoidable first gateway through which addicted individuals must pass on the road to recovery.

PHYSICAL CHANGES IN EARLY RECOVERY

"When Derek got into treatment, I was expecting a changed person," Sandra said of her husband. "Well, he changed all right. He was a wreck."

Derek, a construction worker who had battled alcohol and cocaine addiction for fourteen years, had entered an intensive outpatient program after his second arrest for driving under the influence. He was serious about getting clean, and Sandra, his high school sweetheart and wife of sixteen years, was right there cheering him on.

But he ran into some unexpected problems. His digestive system was a mess. He had aches and pains that he'd never felt before. He couldn't sleep. The nights seemed to stretch on forever, leaving him increasingly agitated and exhausted.

Derek and Sandra didn't realize it at first, but his body was going through an extended period of adjustment—not the immediate intense withdrawal associated with the abrupt cessation of substances, but the often-lengthy process of resetting the body's chemistry.

Anyone who is addicted to a substance of abuse will undergo physical and psychological symptoms of distress when the substance is withheld. For example, when people try to quit smoking cigarettes, they are likely to experience nicotine cravings, irritability, insomnia, fatigue, headaches, and inability to concentrate—all symptoms of nicotine withdrawal.

Acute symptoms of withdrawal can be extremely stressful. Symptoms are likely to be the exact opposite of the effects produced by the substances themselves. For example, withdrawal from stimulants, such as amphetamines and cocaine, generally induces an immediate "crash"—a period of intense exhaustion. Withdrawal from opiates, which ease pain and induce calm, is characterized by nausea, chills, muscle and bone pain, insomnia, and agitation. Alcohol, a depressant that initially acts as a stimulant by suppressing inhibitory functions within the brain, causes withdrawal symptoms similar to those associated with both stimulants and opiates.

As unpleasant as acute withdrawal is, its symptoms are relatively short-lived, often lasting a week or two. But the body must continue to adjust to abstinence. While the symptoms experienced during the months of postwithdrawal are less severe than during acute withdrawal, they are nonetheless distressing and discouraging. To make matters worse, the symptoms last a long time.

A vice president of clinical services at a well-known treatment facility noted, "The body's struggle with the absence of chemicals can last for months. Chemicals change brain chemistry, and the whole ability to manage stress is compromised. People often feel irritable, emotionally and physically unstable. One woman who was addicted to benzodiazepines said that even after nine months in recovery she still felt like her skin was raw—that it was all nerve endings."

Aches and pains are common, as are digestive problems, including constipation and diarrhea. The appetite is also likely to be affected, with some people having little interest in food and others finding themselves eating voraciously. One woman reported, "It was like I exchanged my heroin addiction for food addiction. I never felt full."

Adding to the strain of these physiological changes is another, and even more challenging, aspect of early recovery: sleep disturbances.

The Prevalence of Insomnia

"I don't think Derek slept more than two hours a night for months," Sandra said of her husband's early sobriety. "He'd get up in the middle of the night and go out on the deck and have a cigarette. Or I'd hear him downstairs watching TV. Of course, I was worried about him, so I didn't get much sleep, either. It was tough."

Early recovery has long been associated with sleep disorders, and research into the impact of sleep deprivation on recovery is ongoing. What is known is that sleep is important to the health of our central nervous system, cardiovascular system, immune system, memory, and information processing. Insomnia can lead to fatigue, muscle aches, decreased alertness, poor concentration, depression, and emotional instability. Sleep is as essential for normal human functioning as air, food, and water.

Normal sleep encompasses predictable patterns of brain wave activity. The sleep cycle involves the interaction of many different neurotransmitters, including serotonin, norepinephrine, and dopamine—all of which are affected by addictive substances.

Dopamine, in particular, has been shown to play a key role in regulating brain activity during sleep. In studies involving genetically engineered mice, neuroscientists found that the lack of dopamine completely suppressed brain activity associated with quiet sleep and dreaming. In fact, when dopamine levels were dramatically reduced, the mice could no longer sleep.

Substances of abuse severely deplete the level of dopamine in the brain's reward system. It can take months—and in some cases years—for equilibrium to be reestablished.

One clinician noted, "We might think that insomnia's not such a big deal. We're all sleep deprived to some degree. But sleep deprivation is serious, especially when the body is going through the stress of early sobriety. It can put people at significant risk for relapse."

Her observations are backed up by the New York State Office of Alcoholism and Substance Abuse Services, which states on its Web site: "Physicians and clinicians need to be aware of the growing body of evidence that exists about the relationship between substances of abuse and sleep disorders and they must recognize that when diagnosed and treated effectively, treating sleep disorders in those with addictions can improve their chances of recovery."[2]

Ray, a counselor in a halfway house since overcoming a twenty-five-year heroin addiction eight years ago, said, "The biggest complaint I get from residents here is they can't shut off their mind. It doesn't rest. And it's constantly in overdrive.

"And what I can compare it to is a superhighway of thoughts going two hundred miles an hour. You can't latch on to any of it. You can't stop it, and you can't grab hold of any of it."

Racing thoughts, agitation, and exhaustion are all associated with insomnia—an unhappy legacy of substance abuse. Although insomnia presents a significant stress factor in early recovery, there is no easy solution to the problem. Physical exercise, a healthy diet, and a regular bedtime routine can help. But often it is a long time before sleep patterns become normalized, and there is little to be done other than to wait it out.

As Sandra put it, "The first time Derek slept through the night, it felt like a major victory. We couldn't believe it. And even though he went through a long stretch of not sleeping well after that, we knew it was going to get better. We just had to hang in there."

PSYCHOLOGICAL CHANGES IN EARLY RECOVERY

In *Days of Wine and Roses,* a 1962 movie about a middle-class couple's descent into alcoholism, there's a scene in which a worn-out and listless Kirsten (Lee Remick) tries to explain to her estranged husband, Joe (Jack Lemmon), why she's not interested in joining him in trying to get sober:

"You see, the world looks so dirty to me when I'm not drinking. Joe, remember Fisherman's Wharf? The water when you looked too close? That's the way the world looks to me when I'm not drinking."

It's a heartbreaking scene that captures both the physical toll of addiction and the fundamental psychological challenge of recovery: facing the world on its own terms, warts and all, without the numbing effects of substances.

Addiction is primarily a disease of escape—escape from emotions, responsibility, and everyday reality. Addicts live in a parallel world in which the typical concerns of day-to-day life—family, work, personal growth—take a backseat to the primary activity of getting and using substances. Many addicts begin abusing substances as young teenagers, when the natural course is to develop emotional maturity and coping skills. Relying on drugs to ease pain or to create joy, their emotional growth is often stunted. One rule of thumb is that addicts' emotional age is equivalent to their age when they began using substances. Catching up in terms of emotional and social functioning can take many months and even years of recovery.

In early recovery, addicts begin to experience feelings that have long been suppressed by their substances of choice. Since they have little experience of coping with difficult emotions, their psychological challenges can be daunting.

As one counselor put it, "People look at themselves and ask, *What have I done? I have done these terrible things. What kind of person am I?* These are difficult questions for anyone to face. But learning to express them and cope with them is one of the basic tasks of recovery."

Cravings are among the first feelings to assault a brain deprived of its accustomed chemicals. The intense, all-consuming desire for substances can occur seemingly out of nowhere, but it is often an automatic response to an uncomfortable emotion.

Tara, a twenty-eight-year-old recovering heroin addict, said, "Emotions are hard. Being totally sober, not being numb at all, just having to sit in my skin was hard. Every time you have an emotion, you think about using."

Cravings are the conditioned response of a brain that has learned to associate substances with relief from discomfort. And they're a significant challenge for people who are getting sober. "People are sometimes afraid of their cravings," noted one counselor. "They might be doing really well, and then out of nowhere comes this incredible urge to pick up again. It can be frightening. But everyone who successfully overcomes addiction has to learn how to tolerate the cravings without using."

Fortunately, cravings weaken over time as addicts acquire new coping skills. But they are far from the only source of anxiety in early recovery. Handling anger can be a significant challenge for many addicts.

Facing Up to Anger
The physical strain of postwithdrawal is likely to compromise addicts' ability to take things in stride. Their emotions are raw and their coping skills shaky. Minor annoyances can be blown out of proportion, and everyday challenges can create significant distress. It may take a lot of practice before addicts learn how to handle anger appropriately. And we, as family members, may need to find better ways of responding to anger.

Cheryl, whose husband has been sober for thirteen months, has grown increasingly distressed by his angry outbursts. "Everything can be fine," she said, "and then some little thing will set him off. If we're in the car and the person in front of us doesn't go the second the light turns green, or if someone in the grocery store holds up the checkout line, he'll fume for hours. Last week he blew up at our daughter because she lost one of her gloves. You'd have thought it was the end of the world."

She hesitated before adding, "I know addiction is a disease. At least, I think I believe that. But it's hard to have sympathy for someone who makes everyone around him miserable. And it's hard to bite my tongue when he's being a jerk."

Cheryl's mistake is in believing that because addiction is a disease, the addict is not responsible for his behavior. Nothing could be further from the truth. Her husband is undoubtedly under a lot of stress, but one of his primary tasks in recovery is to take responsibility for his actions. Active addicts blame other people for their problems. People in recovery learn to hold themselves accountable.

Cheryl does neither her husband nor herself any good by accepting unacceptable behavior. She may need professional help to find effective ways of letting her husband know that there are behaviors she won't tolerate. She may also need practice overlooking minor annoyances and "not going to every fight she's invited to," to put it in AA terms.

Her husband's anger is a significant issue that needs to be addressed before real progress in recovery can be made.

No More Running

Ed, a recovering alcoholic who has been a counselor in a residential program almost twenty years, said, "Everyone who comes in here is afraid. They're fearful about what to expect. They're afraid of living without substances. They're afraid they won't make it. When the younger ones meet guys who have been through this over and over again, they're afraid that'll be them. We tell them it doesn't have to be that way. Sometimes people do make it on the first or second try."

Fear, so common in early recovery, is a big part of addiction itself. Addicts don't escape into substances because they're good at facing things. Instead, their inclination is to avoid problems, to run away from difficulties. Until he found sobriety, said Ray, "I spent a lifetime running, running. And I don't know what the hell I was running from."

Tara said, "The hardest thing about not using is you can no longer run. You can't just run away anymore."

Kevin, a thirty-nine-year-old recovering alcoholic with nine months of sobriety, observed, "Running is a big part of addiction. It takes a while to learn that it's okay to feel your feelings. It's okay to cry."

On the face of it, it might seem strange to think of addicts as fearful people. After all, they take risks with their lives that most of us would find terrifying. My own daughter would cruise the streets of the worst neighborhoods in search for drugs. Every time she stuck a needle in her arm, she risked dying. Yet she was unable to cope with the possibility of rejection and incapable of allowing anyone to get close to her. Like many addicts, my daughter's reaction to emotions was to run away from them.

When addicts decide to stop running and try to get clean, they begin to expose their vulnerability. This can be a frightening prospect.

Ed said of his early days in the halfway house where he found sobriety, "I was so frightened when I first came here that after ten days I asked to go back to jail. I didn't want to speak in AA meetings. I didn't know what to say if I wasn't putting on an act. The hardest thing for me was getting honest with myself. When I was drinking, the walls were up. Before you can get better, they have to come down."

Tara also struggled with expressing her feelings. After six years in recovery, she said, "I still have a hard time talking at meetings. I have a hard time opening up. There are certain areas that at first I felt ashamed of: prostitution, things like that. Even now, a lot of times I wish I could just drink. But I have to open up if I want to stay clean."

Being vulnerable and expressing our feelings is hard for most of us. No one likes getting hurt or rejected, and owning our mistakes and shortcomings can be a struggle. For addicts, dealing with emotions is made more challenging by the heavy burden of guilt and regret they so often carry. Over the course of their addiction, they are likely to have suffered enormous losses and inflicted pain on the people who love them most.

Somehow, their most painful emotions must be faced during the process of recovery.

Counting the Losses

There are probably few people in this world who, when looking back over their lives, don't have at least some regrets—missed opportunities, damaged relationships, or unfulfilled dreams. For people with addictions, the common mistakes of the human experience are magnified by the distorting power of chemicals. As the numbing effects of substances wear off in early sobriety, addicts often awaken to a sense of enormous loss and overwhelming shame.

Coming to terms with the damage done may take years, rather than months, but the seeds for healing are planted in early recovery.

In his youth, Kevin was a gifted operatic singer with a strong spiritual inclination. He explored the possibility of entering the priesthood. He was also a talented mason who enjoyed working with his hands. "While I was trying to figure out what to do with my life, it kept sliding downhill," he reflected. "I went from owning my own condo to living in my parents' basement to renting a room in the YMCA. I told myself, *It's okay. It's a nice room.*"

By the age of thirty-nine, he was drinking a gallon of brandy a day and living on multivitamins. "I got so I could drink enough to pass out and wake up in time for my favorite TV shows," he said. "It was a sad life."

One day, he passed out in the hallway near the bathroom, where a fellow resident found him. He had bleeding esophageal varices, a life-threatening condition in which the arteries and veins rupture as a result of liver damage. He almost died.

"I was scared to death," he recalled. "I had the sense of being such a loser. I'd amounted to nothing over the years. I mean, all the lost opportunities. All the waste. How could I drink myself to death? I was very angry for months."

Richy, a recovering alcoholic who has been sober three years, also looks back on squandered opportunities. As an adolescent, he was a superb athlete. His skill on the football field earned him full scholarships to a prestigious prep school and several colleges. He enjoyed staying in shape and prided himself on being a fierce competitor.

But in college, his life began to revolve around alcohol and cocaine. Instead of finishing college, he landed a job in the construction trade, got married, and had two kids. His drinking steadily increased, but he was functioning—even when he had to down a six-pack every morning before heading to work.

In time, his marriage broke up. He lost everything, including contact with his children, and wound up living on the streets. With his life on the line, Richy decided to get sober. Looking back, he said, "It was hard to accept everything I'd lost. It was hard to face the consequences of my actions. I'm still taking it one day at a time."

For Tara, the overdose death of her high school sweetheart was her greatest loss. "He was the love of my life," she said. "I was high at his wake. I kept trying to cry, but I had some heroin in my car, and that was all I could think about. I wanted to go out and get it. It makes you totally numb to everything. Nothing matters. I didn't want to experience the feelings of my boyfriend being dead. I didn't deal with that for a long time."

When she finally decided to get clean—after twenty previous attempts—she experienced the grief she had put off feeling for years.

The Burden of Shame

In addition to loss and regret, many addicts in early recovery experience a painful sense of shame. One counselor told me that she believes guilt and shame are among the biggest obstacles to recovery. "People can come to believe that they don't deserve a better life," she explained. "They can feel that they've done too much damage, that they're bad people. When they aren't able to work through those feelings of shame, there's little motivation for them to get clean."

Eight years into his recovery, Ray continues to struggle with guilt about the way he treated his family, especially his mother and grandmother. "I took advantage of the people who cared about me the most," he admitted. "Twenty-five years ago, my mom would jokingly say things like, 'You're going to make me gray before my time.' Today, she is very unhealthy, and I blame myself. She's a white-haired woman, and I blame myself for every gray hair on her head."

An especially painful memory involves his grandmother. "I had a very loving grandmother," he recalled. "She was my rock. Whenever I went to jail, I'd send her letters, and she'd always write me back. Always. She was on social security, but she'd always send me ten dollars, whatever. I ended up robbing her and letting my cousin take the blame."

The memory still brings tears to his eyes. Although he tries to make up for his past by "being the best son I can be, the best person I can be," Ray said, "My grandmother passed away shortly before I got clean. That's one amend I haven't been able to make."

Judy, a recovering crack addict and former prostitute, lost custody of her two young children when she was twenty-three. She spent the next twelve years running away from her deep sense of loss and shame. "Every time I tried to get clean, I'd have to face what I had done to those two innocent kids. I couldn't take it," she said. "I mean, how does any mother give up her babies?"

It was only after a second failed suicide attempt that she got into a treatment program that helped her come to terms with her past. In time, she said, "I learned that I wasn't a bad person. I was a person who had done bad things. And that meant I was also a person who could do good things if I chose to."

Judy decided to get serious about recovery. "I can't change the past and all the harm I've done to my kids. That's something I'll have to live with the rest of my life," she explained. "But I can try to be a better person."

In the tradition of the Twelve Steps, Judy is learning to cope with her feelings of shame by admitting her mistakes and trying to make amends to the people she has hurt. And like many addicts, the people she has hurt the most are the people who loved her the most.

THE FAMILY'S PAIN

It may come as a surprise to some people to discover that their addicted loved ones have feelings of regret, sorrow, and shame. After all, addiction is the most selfish of diseases. Addicts will typically lie, steal, cheat, and generally run roughshod over anyone who stands in their way of the next drink or fix. They show little consideration for anyone else's feelings and don't seem to care how much pain they inflict.

Their apparent lack of feelings is a consequence of (as well as motivator for) chemical addiction. Even if, deep inside, they don't like themselves very much, the easy remedy of chemical oblivion takes away the emotional discomfort. Only as recovery progresses do they come face to face with painful feelings they have long suppressed.

Their families, on the other hand, have suffered repeatedly during the years of active addiction. We have watched in agony as promising young lives are ruined. We have suffered repeated heart-aches as promises are broken. We have been shocked to discover that someone we love has robbed us, conned us, used our good intentions as a way to score drugs. And we have paced through many long nights, not knowing if our loved one is alive or dead.

When our loved one decides to get clean, we may find ourselves confronting some difficult emotions of our own.

"I was so angry at my daughter that I didn't speak to her the whole first year of her recovery," one mother recalled. "She'd left her children with us and took off for eight months. In all that time, she called maybe five times, and then it was only to ask for money. Then she gets clean and expects to come waltzing back into our lives? I had a hard time with that one."

A wife said of her husband's lengthy treatment program, "He went off to take care of his problems and left me holding the bag. I had to deal with the fallout, the kids, the bills, the house, the gossip. When he finally came home, I was furious."

Another woman said, "Yes, I'm grateful that's he's sober today. But what about the fifteen years of hell he put us through?"

Anger is a normal response to people who hurt and take advantage of us. And like our addicted loved one, we may have difficulty coming to terms with our anger.

Psychologists tell us we have a right to our feelings, that feelings in themselves are not wrong. It is only our actions that have consequences. One of the most effective ways to deal with anger is to cultivate forgiveness. But that can be a long time coming in the early, sometimes tumultuous, days of recovery.

As if to add insult to injury, most of us are not only angry, we are also disappointed. We may find that sobriety alone is not a cure-all. It does not magically change our loved ones into the people we had hoped they would be. Characteristics we may have attributed to the effects of substances may be, in fact, inherent character traits. (There's an old AA saying that goes, "When a horse thief gets clean, you've still got a horse thief.") A sloppy housekeeper or a person who was careless with money, for example, may continue to show those traits in recovery. As the blurring effects of chemicals wear off, we may not like everything we see.

We may also be disappointed to learn that early recovery does not put everything back on track—at least not in our minds. One woman, for example, was dismayed to learn that her son, a talented artist, had decided to drop out of college and become a chef. A man was disturbed to learn that his wife, a nurse, was no longer willing to continue working in her field. The parents of a young mother were heartbroken when their daughter voluntarily surrendered custody of her children to her ex-husband.

"All that potential, all that promise, gone for nothing," we are apt to think when the full aftermath of addiction begins to dawn on us. Even though recovery can bring our loved one a richer, more meaningful life than anything we might have imagined—and even though those we love have the right to determine their own destiny—it takes a while for us to achieve that awareness.

To further complicate matters, our emotional turmoil may be intensified by the persistence of fear.

Replacing Fear with Acceptance
I remember a friend of mine breaking down in tears a few years ago. Her husband was coming home after a month of inpatient treatment, to be followed by an intensive outpatient program. "I'm happy because I miss him," she said between sobs. "But I'm scared. I'm afraid all the bad stuff will start all over."

I did my best to be encouraging, but I understood her fear. For many of us who have lived with addiction, fear becomes a kind of constant companion, not always in our consciousness but never far beneath the surface. We fear getting the phone call that tells us our loved one has been arrested, has been in an accident, or has died. We fear that the unhappiness and constant crises will never end.

We can become so accustomed to living with fear that it may dominate our thoughts when recovery begins. Instead of feeling relief at this positive development in our loved one's life, we may find ourselves filled with apprehension. We may ask ourselves, *How will recovery affect our relationship? What if I get my hopes up and then it doesn't work out? What if things get even worse?*

As understandable as these reactions are, it's helpful to remember that the "what ifs" of life rob us of the ability to appreciate the present. It is only by living in the day—even the moment—that we can attain the peace of mind we truly deserve.

We cannot force our loved ones to find recovery, and we cannot control the process or the outcome. What we can do is accept life as it is at this moment, without dwelling on the past or projecting into the future. We can accept that emotional turmoil and unresolved issues are an inevitable part of early recovery—for both our loved one and ourselves. We can accept that it's okay to have unanswered questions.

Most of all, we can accept our loved one and ourselves as we are and where we are in these early days of a long process. Acceptance—that is, acknowledging the reality of what is—is the starting point from which emotional healing can begin.

TIPS FOR DEALING WITH THE PHYSICAL AND PSYCHOLOGICAL CHALLENGES OF EARLY RECOVERY

Supporting the Addict

1. Respect the struggle. Your loved one has entered a period of intense physical and emotional upheaval. Acknowledge the challenges.
2. Encourage your loved one to take care of her physical health—but avoid nagging her about it.
3. Do not blame or shame. Your loved one knows he has harmed himself and others. That is already his burden to bear and come to terms with.

4. Accept your loved one for where she is now in her journey. She may still have a long way to go in terms of personal growth. Recognize that the path is long.

5. Keep things in perspective. Your loved one has not had much practice in dealing with difficult emotions. Before making an issue out of something, ask yourself if it is a minor annoyance that will pass. Ask yourself, how important is it?

Supporting Yourself

1. Get professional support. Addiction has caused enormous pain and suffering. Working through these difficult emotions is faster and easier with help.

2. Take care of your health. Stress can negatively impact physical well-being. Do what you need to do to stay (or get) healthy.

3. Do not accept abuse of any kind. Make your physical, emotional, and financial boundaries clear. The emotional turmoil of early recovery does not excuse abusive behavior.

4. Cultivate forgiveness. Holding on to anger and resentment damages relationships. More important, it diminishes your ability to enjoy life.

5. Let go of what might have been. Regret is an energy drainer. Accept the current reality. Only by accepting what is can things begin to change.

CHAPTER 3

✣

FINDING PLACE AND PURPOSE

*Whatever is at the center of our life will be the source
of our security, guidance, wisdom, and power.*
—STEPHEN COVEY

"Our son would steal anything that wasn't nailed down," Mike says matter-of-factly. "It got to the point where we took out a restraining order on him. We couldn't have him around."

I remember his son as a slender, blond child who'd been in the same class as my daughter in elementary school. After Mike and his family moved out of town, we'd lost touch—until fate brought us together again at a Nar-Anon meeting.

Mike sips his coffee and shakes his head. "Who would've guessed?"

I know what he means. My living room, where he has come to talk to me about his son, is filled with photographs that chronicle my daughter's progression from radiant little girl to somber young woman.

"Anyway, he came home four months ago," Mike continues. "First time he's lived at home in—oh, six years. We were kind of nervous about it. But he's clean and he didn't have any place else to go, and we wanted to give him a chance . . ."

He pauses and looks away, as if he's a little embarrassed by what he's about to say. "It's been hard on all of us," Mike admits. "I mean, we're happy to have him there, of course. But, well, you know how mothers are. I think Cindy was expecting we'd be one big, happy family again. Just kind of pick up where we left off when he was a kid. But it's not like that. It's almost like he's—I don't know. A stranger."

I glance at a picture of my daughter. She's around sixteen, standing outside the house with the pink rhododendrons in full glorious bloom behind her. She's laughing at the camera as if she hasn't a care in the world, but I wonder what secrets she was hiding even then.

"He's so different," Mike continues. "He doesn't say much. He doesn't seem to have any ambition. He goes to his meetings and works a minimum wage job stocking shelves. That's about the extent of it. And his mother and I walk around on eggshells because we don't want to do anything that might upset him."

He scratches his head. "I mean, you'd think that after six months in a program and four months at home he'd have made more progress than this. I'm beginning to wonder if things will ever get back to normal."

It's a reasonable question, and he thinks a moment before coming up with an answer himself. "I guess we just have to give it time."

THE SOCIAL COSTS OF ADDICTION

In the early days and weeks of our loved one's recovery, most of us are willing to cut her a little slack. We may avoid doing things we think will upset her. We may tell ourselves to be patient when her moods fluctuate for no apparent reason. After the turmoil of active addiction, we may eagerly try to create an environment we hope will support recovery.

Eventually, however, we want life to settle down. We want to be able to be ourselves—warts and all—around our recovering loved one. We want the uncertainties of early recovery to fade away. And it can be frustrating when the return to normalcy (however we define it) is a long time coming.

The difficulty stems from the fact that it has typically been a long time since our addict behaved in a mature, responsible way. He may have a hard time functioning in a social setting without his drug of choice. Because addiction stunts emotional growth, his ability to interact with others—including family members and the broader community—may be severely impaired.

For many active addicts, "normal" behavior implies dishonesty, manipulation, isolation, and self-centeredness to the exclusion of all else. Unlearning those behaviors and acquiring the necessary skills to become functioning members of society can be a long, hard road indeed.

The Secret Self

Swiss psychiatrist Carl Jung (1875–1961) devoted much of his work to exploring the "dark side" of human beings—that is, the shadowy, subconscious self that harbors our deepest fears and most negative impulses. According to Jung, we all have a shadow self that is markedly different from the self we reveal to the world— different, even, from our own concept of who we are.

Jung believed that our dark side casts a long shadow over our relationships and life choices. He theorized that we are destined to repeat the same mistakes time and again until we shed the light of awareness on our shadow self and thus diminish its power. Only by admitting the existence of our weaknesses—by facing our demons head-on—can we limit their influence over us.

Whether we subscribe to Jung's ideas about the "dark side," there is little doubt that most of us have aspects of ourselves that we would rather not expose to the light of day. We have thoughts or impulses that we're not exactly proud of and that we share with very few people—if anyone at all.

People addicted to alcohol and other drugs take the concept of the shadow self to an extreme level. Because addiction can incur severe social, financial, and legal consequences, budding addicts quickly learn to hide evidence of their substance abuse and the life they've built around it. They lie about where they are and what they are doing. They create fictitious explanations for their erratic behavior. They build a secret life perpetuated by dishonesty, deflection, and denial. My daughter is a case in point.

For several years, she worked as a nurse's aide. She was good at it. She liked her elderly clients, and they liked her. Her nurse supervisor thought highly of her and encouraged her to get a nursing degree.

I, too, was proud of her work. But I worried constantly about what she was up to between the time she got out of work at three in the afternoon and the time she got home, usually around nine-thirty at night. She offered vague explanations having to do with going shopping or driving around "to relax."

One night, she got arrested in a "shooting gallery"—a place where addicts go to get high. The full extent of her double life came out: conscientious aide by day, drug addict by night. Lying had become second nature to her—far easier than telling the truth. She had put up walls to prevent anyone from getting close and guarded her secret existence with unflagging vigilance.

The result, of course, was that she drove away her friends and became alienated from her family. She lost her job and was unable to find another one. Her social network dwindled to using buddies who were incapable of having a genuine relationship with her.

The secret life my daughter constructed to support her addiction led her to a very lonely place. But it was more than secrets that fed her growing isolation. It was the addiction itself.

A Party of One

Addiction is sometimes associated with a "party" lifestyle. The image of beer-guzzling frat boys and drug-dazed club-goers has become a fixture in the entertainment industry, promoting the perception that exhilarating social interaction is an inevitable by-product of intoxication. And for many people who become addicted, there is some truth in that perception. My daughter recalled that in her early days of smoking pot, she and her best friend could "just lie on our backs and watch the clouds and laugh our asses off about nothing." A recovering alcoholic said, "We drank because it was fun. It was fun for all of us at first. If it wasn't, we wouldn't have kept doing it."

When occasional drug use progresses to regular use and then addiction, the "fun" disappears. Social occasions become just another opportunity to pursue a solitary high. The alcoholic at a wedding focuses primarily on getting more drinks without anyone noticing. The addict at the graduation party disappears repeatedly to take drugs and maintain the chemical high. Family and nonaddicted friends take a backseat to drinking and drugging buddies.

In time, the inevitable social consequence of addiction is isolation and alienation.

Kevin, who nearly drank himself to death by the age of thirty-nine, described himself as having three friends: "the television, the remote, and the bottle." Richy, who managed to hold a job during much of his alcoholism, remembered his life as consisting of "coming home from work and shutting myself in my apartment with a case of beer." Pat, whose drinking escalated after retirement, found that her children stopped visiting her in the evenings because by then she'd be drunk. And Calvin, who typically downed a twelve-pack while watching sports with his family and friends, felt increasingly alone even in a crowd.

Even drinking and drugging buddies are not likely to be friends in any meaningful sense. Instead, as one young woman explained, "They're using buddies." After being three months sober in a court-mandated inpatient program, she said, "When I was first here, I called everyone I knew. When they heard I wasn't using anymore, it would be 'click.' Not one of my so-called friends has called to ask how I'm doing."

When there is simply no source of pleasure other than the chemical high, there is little motivation—or ability—to build nurturing relationships. Social connections center on getting and using substances rather than on genuine caring, respect, or interest.

Furthermore, as interactions with the sober world become less frequent, addicts begin to view themselves as outsiders, as misfits who can't blend into the social fabric. And as addiction itself triggers increasingly unconventional behavior, society's response is likely to reinforce this perception.

SOCIETY'S OUTCASTS

Most of us tend to think of our addicted loved one as a good person who made bad choices. During the years of active addiction, we are likely to remember him as he was before addiction took hold and to remind ourselves of his positive qualities. Even if the addiction leads to extreme behavior that leaves us feeling bitter and alienated, we are inclined to see our loved one as a fundamentally decent person who has been altered by addiction.

Society's view of our loved one, however, may be much less benign.

The antisocial behaviors associated with substance abuse can turn addicts into social outcasts. Tara, a petite young woman with clear skin and shiny hair, described her former life as an active addict:

> I'd hang out in front of stores and pretend I was raising money for a charity. It worked because I look so innocent. I also stole a lot. I stole meat at grocery stores and sold it at bars for half price. I stole baseball cards and sold them at a card shop. The first time I was a prostitute was at this baseball card shop. The owner was basically a dirty old man. I gave him sex for money. Pretty soon I started walking around the streets and guys would give

me a look. They'd give me money for sex. Four to six times a day I'd do that, and my boyfriend would do what he had to do—steal, rob people.

In those days, Tara said, people often called her a "scumbag" and other humiliating names. They would look at her with contempt, "like I was something disgusting." Ray, a counselor in a residential program, had a similar experience. During his years of addiction, he said:

I was a thief, an incredible thief. I lived by shoplifting, conning. I also reaped the benefits from prostitutes in the city. I had a female cousin. For many years, I would protect her when she was working the streets, take down license numbers so if she didn't come back, I knew where to look for her. I took 50 percent of her money.

In time, Ray said, he encountered scorn and rejection on a daily basis. "Strangers in the street would see me and say, 'We need to avoid that guy,'" he explained. "Your health goes out the window. Your personal pride goes out the window. Your hygiene goes out the window. Your morals go out the window. Your eyes look like a wolf's on the prowl. And that's what I turned into."

Lynn, a nurse who was addicted to prescription drugs, got hostile looks from her co-workers as the quality of her patient care slipped. Her boss threatened to fire her if she didn't start showing up on time. The girls she used to go to "happy hour" with stopped asking her to join them after she repeatedly became embarrassingly loud and obnoxious. She said, "I lost the respect and friendship of the people I cared most about."

Shannon, a crack addict who had worked in a strip club, recalled, "Wherever I went, people's heads would turn. I told myself it was because I was hot. Now I know it's because I looked disgusting."

Being on the receiving end of contempt and rejection hurts—even people who claim not to care. Even through the fog of addiction.

As family members, we hope that with the onset of sobriety, the person we used to know will reemerge—maybe a little scarred, hopefully a little wiser—ready and eager to rejoin society full-steam ahead.

What takes time for many of us to realize, however, is that addiction has profoundly changed our loved one's view of herself. Her self-confidence and self-respect have been severely shaken. She has done things she is deeply ashamed of and encountered repeated blows to her self-esteem. Even if her addiction has not resulted in loss of job, home, or social status, she may have come to identify herself as a social outsider.

Addicts in early recovery are faced with redefining their role in society. They must reassess who they are and figure out how to fit into the social structure. One valuable tool for doing this is through participation in Twelve Step programs.

Alcoholics Anonymous, Narcotics Anonymous, and similar support groups provide a ready-made, positive social network. In Twelve Step meetings, recovering addicts meet people who have had experiences similar to their own. They find understanding and acceptance, which reduces the terrible sting of "not fitting in." And within the framework of a nonjudgmental environment, they begin to develop the necessary skills for building meaningful relationships.

The process of mending the social fabric is likely to be slow and difficult. But the support provided by Twelve Step programs can go a long way toward helping our loved one learn how to become a functioning, responsible member of society.

WORKING TO BELONG

Linda and her husband, Dave, had a good life. She ran a bridal shop, and he was a well-known physician with a large private practice. High school sweethearts with three healthy children and a lovely home, they had been married twenty-five years when a long-held secret turned their lives upside down.

"He went out for Chinese food one Christmas Eve and didn't come home," Linda recalled. "I got a call from the police station saying they had arrested him for writing false prescriptions."

At first, she thought they were crazy, that it was all a mistake. But she quickly learned that her husband had been hiding a long-standing addiction to opiates. "When you're a physician, you have access to anything you want," she said.

He went into a treatment program for addicted physicians and, eight months later, resumed his family practice. After three years, he relapsed. When he returned from treatment this time, he announced that he was not ready for full-time work.

"He said that he would never practice medicine again," Linda recalled. "He said it was too much stress and he couldn't handle it. So he didn't work at all the first ninety days he was home—just attended meetings. Then he did substitute teaching in high school for a year. Then he got a job in a summer prep school program. Then he was a visiting professor at a college."

All the time, Linda recalled, he was making very little money. Her resentment began to grow. "We'd gone through our savings to pay for his treatments. We had one kid in college and two others getting ready to go. He'd left me to deal with all the fallout from his addiction, the bills, the forms, the publicity. And he was too stressed to do what he was trained for? I was angry."

Her reaction was not unreasonable. After all, she had endured enormous strain because of her husband's actions and done everything within her power to keep the household afloat. In effect, she had been left holding the bag while he focused on his personal recovery. Surely it was reasonable to expect that once he was clean and sober, he would return to work and begin earning the income their family required.

Her husband was simply not ready. He had completed an

excellent treatment program, he was clean, and he was eager to put addiction behind him. But he was uncertain of his ability to cope with stress. He was also reluctant to place himself in an environment where addictive substances were part of the landscape, admitting to himself that he might not be able to resist temptation.

In time, Linda came to recognize that her husband's low-paying jobs were part of his long-term recovery process. "He needed a few years away from medicine to really clear his head," she said. "I wasn't happy about it, but it's what he needed to do."

Dave eventually began practicing medicine again, at first on a part-time per diem basis and later as a full-time practitioner in an urban hospital. Like many other recovering addicts, he recognized that having a job was an important piece of reintegrating into society. But, also like many others, his return to work was complicated and fraught with challenges.

The Value of Work

Work (whether paid or unpaid) is highly valued in our society. Our sense of identity and purpose is influenced by the work we do. Our sense of self-worth is strengthened by our work-related contributions to the community. And our sense of belonging is nurtured when we are part of a group of people with shared goals and responsibilities.

For recovering addicts, the value of work has added dimensions. One important benefit of work is that it adds structure to the day. Many addicted individuals exist in a shapeless landscape of vast stretches of empty time. Other than pursuing and using alcohol and other drugs, they have little to do. Having a job helps addicts adjust to the social rhythm of their community and provides a useful framework for managing their time.

Another important benefit of work is that it teaches personal responsibility. Addiction almost always results in erratic, irresponsible behavior. As employees, however, recovering addicts are expected to show up on time, follow the rules, and complete assigned tasks.

Finally, work promotes recovery because it can contribute to self-esteem. Work allows addicts to begin to reclaim control over their lives (which have been alarmingly out of control). It provides an opportunity to contribute to society—even if that contribution is as simple as serving coffee or cleaning floors. And it promotes a sense of being capable and competent to deal with life's challenges, essential components of healthy self-esteem.

Despite the many benefits of work, finding a job can be challenging for individuals with poor work histories, criminal records, or inadequate skills. Many recovering addicts require work skills training, and many reenter the workforce in low-level, low-paid positions.

One counselor observed, "Some guys feel like they lower themselves by taking a job at eight dollars an hour. Some of these guys had a good job. They have a mortgage, families. But even if they had this stuff, it wasn't working for them, because they're in a halfway house. You feel for them, but they can't have the money they used to have right away. They have to rebuild."

Poor self-esteem and poor social skills can present additional obstacles to finding work. My daughter, for example, was unable to return to work in the medical field because of her record of drug possession. Having no other job skills, she decided to take courses at a community college. Two months after enrolling, she dropped out. When I asked why she had quit, her answer was vague: "I don't know. I got a sixty-nine on a history test and I just didn't go back." She also mentioned feeling uncomfortable around other students. "I didn't know I would feel so different," she said.

She decided to look for a job. But each of the prospects she told me about came to nothing. In time, she admitted that she couldn't bring herself to go to the interviews. "Sometimes I sit in the parking lot and think, *Why would they hire me?*" she confessed. "And then I just drive away."

Was my daughter more easily defeated or more negative than other recovering addicts? Were her thought processes unusually distorted? I don't think so.

A psychiatrist described early recovery as a period of "emotional rawness." "People are extremely sensitive," he said. "Things that may seem insignificant later on can trigger intense emotional reactions in that early stage."

A counselor in a group home for women described the biggest challenge of early recovery—aside from the obsession to use—as "getting out of the fog" that comes with addiction. "Thinking isn't clear. Self-perception is twisted," she said. "The fog of self-defeating thoughts can be overwhelming, and it can take months, sometimes years, for that fog to lift."

Although the value of work in reintegrating addicts into society is undeniable, finding work presents a significant challenge for many individuals in early recovery. It may take a combination of training and professional counseling—as well as encouragement and patience from family members—before this important step is finally achieved.

SPIRITUALITY MATTERS

Western medicine is increasingly recognizing the value of spirituality in the healing process. Studies have found that people with strong spiritual beliefs heal faster from surgery, have lower blood pressure, are less anxious and depressed, and cope better with chronic illnesses than their nonspiritual counterparts. Some studies have also linked strong religious beliefs with longevity.

So persuasive is the evidence that spirituality can have a positive impact on health that many medical schools are including spiritual teachings in their curricula. And the importance of spirituality in healing from addiction has been widely recognized for many years.

The role of spirituality in the founding of Alcoholics Anonymous has been well documented. In the 1930s, an alcoholic known as Rowland H. sought help from Carl Jung, who informed his patient that his condition was hopeless "so far as any further medical or psychiatric treatment might be concerned." In a 1961 letter to Jung, AA cofounder Bill Wilson wrote, "This candid and humble statement of yours was beyond doubt the first foundation stone upon which our Society has since been built."

Wilson continued, "When he then asked you if there was any other hope, you told him that there might be, provided he could become the subject of a spiritual or religious experience—in short, a genuine conversion."

As a result of Jung's observation, Rowland H. joined the Oxford Group, an evangelical movement that emphasized "self-survey, confession, restitution, and the giving of oneself in service to others." He found relief from his obsession to drink, and word of his experience eventually spread to Bill Wilson, whose lengthy struggle with alcoholism was later relieved by his own spiritual awakening. He wrote to Jung, "My release from the alcohol obsession was immediate."

"In the wake of my spiritual experience there came a vision of a society of alcoholics, each identifying with and transmitting his experience to the next—chain style," he continued. Near the end of his letter, Wilson added, "Because of your conviction that man is something more than intellect, emotion, and two dollars worth of chemicals, you have especially endeared yourself to us."

In his reply to Wilson, Jung wrote that Rowland H.'s "craving for alcohol was the equivalent on a low level of the spiritual thirst of our being for wholeness, expressed in medieval language: the union with God."

Jung's observation was so profound that it is worth restating: The "craving for alcohol was the equivalent . . . of the spiritual thirst of our being for wholeness."

The sense of being incomplete, fragmented, and empty is a common theme among addicted individuals. In fact, it is widely held that all addictions—whether to substances (including food) or behaviors—are an attempt to fill a void.

The truth of this hit home with me when I was driving my daughter to her first detox. She seemed small and listless beside me, staring without comment out the window. After a long period of silence, she whispered, "I feel so empty inside."

I have heard similar comments from many people in recovery over the years, including twenty-four-year-old Shannon, whose addictions led to six prison stints. "There was all this pain," she recalled. "I was trying to fill a void." Author Nic Sheff, recounting his painful journey through addiction in his book *Tweak,* put it this way: "Still, for all the therapy I had, none of it ever really fixed that feeling of torn-apartness inside of me."[3]

Because addictions are so closely linked to feeling empty, separate, and without purpose, recovery almost always encompasses a strong spiritual component. It is the spiritual element of recovery that offers the greatest hope for sustained personal growth and healing.

Defining Spirituality

Many people equate spirituality with religion. This can make the spiritual element of recovery challenging for those whose early religious experiences were troubling—for example, those who were taught to view God as a purely punitive figure—and for those with no religious beliefs whatsoever.

In fact, the spiritual foundation of Alcoholics Anonymous and other Twelve Step programs has aroused a fair amount of criticism over the years. It is not uncommon to hear addicted individuals complain, "All that God stuff turns me off. I can't relate to all that talk about a Higher Power."

These are statements my own daughter has made. These are sentiments I myself have experienced during Al-Anon or Nar-Anon meetings, especially when I have felt particularly determined to take matters into my own hands. But such resistance generally stems from a misunderstanding about what is meant by "spirituality."

In general terms, spirituality involves the belief in something greater than oneself (a Higher Power), an awareness of purpose in life, a feeling of interconnectedness with others, and the development of personal values.

Although spirituality is often associated with religion, the two are not necessarily interdependent. It is possible to have spiritual beliefs outside the doctrines of any particular religion, just as it is possible to follow religious doctrines without being particularly spiritual. Furthermore, the Twelve Steps—which promote *spiritual,* not *religious,* beliefs—are not the only pathway to spiritual growth as it relates to recovery. Spiritual paths are intensely personal, as varied and individual as the path to recovery itself.

Often the path to spirituality begins with the simple plea for help to resist the urge to use. "I got down on my knees one day and asked my Higher Power to not let me use," one woman recalled. "I didn't believe in anything. I felt stupid. But it worked."

A man with three years of sobriety said, "I ask my Higher Power every morning to help me stay clean, and I thank my Higher Power every night for another day sober."

"Anytime I feel the urge to use, I ask God to please take the urge away," another woman said.

Shannon, in recovery for the first time since she began using drugs at the age of fourteen, described her spiritual journey this way:

> I need to believe in something greater than myself. I had God in my life when I was an addict, but I used him like, "God, please don't let me go to jail. God, please let me get this bag without the cops finding me. God, please let me get this five dollars so I can get this high." And God

wasn't answering my prayers because he doesn't answer selfish prayers like that. He's not going to give you something that's not good for you. And that's where I thought God had left me. But now, by reading the AA literature and the Bible as well, and by giving up my will, I do it different. I say, "God, please teach me how to handle this. God, please help me keep this in the hour." And I'm learning to be happy.

Thirty-nine-year-old Kevin, whose alcoholism nearly killed him, revealed a more unusual spiritual awakening:

I was in the hospital for over a month, and during that time I would get visits from Dr. Dan. The first time he came with two nurses, and he kind of scolded me for what I had done to myself. Then he said, "I saved your life," in a kind way, like a parent would. Every time he came, he was kind and encouraging. When I was leaving the hospital, I asked to speak with Dr. Dan. They said there was no one on their staff by that name. They checked with other hospitals and the register of visitors. No one by that name had come. I pointed to the door that I had seen him go in and out of, but it was just a closet. He didn't exist.

Kevin interpreted the visits from Dr. Dan as a message from his Higher Power. "It was pretty profound," he said. "My life was saved for a reason. It made me want to do something worthwhile with my life, to do something to help people. Today I have sobriety, recovery, and peace."

Developing Spirituality
The earliest records of human activity suggest that the search for meaning has always been a defining characteristic of what it means

to be human. Stone gods and goddesses, cave drawings, and articles placed in burial chambers all point to an innate longing to experience ourselves as something beyond the confines of body and time.

For thousands of years, through ceremony, song, and literature, we have expressed our need for a sense of purpose, for being interconnected with others, and for being part of something greater than ourselves.

These enduring aspects of the human experience are especially important to people in recovery, who so often operate from a place of shame, emptiness, loneliness, and purposelessness. Spirituality allows them to experience themselves as worthwhile people who have something of value to offer society and who are part of a greater whole.

As important as spirituality is to recovery, however, it doesn't always come easily. Instead, it often springs from a place of deep despair. As Nic Sheff wrote:

> I close my eyes, tears streaming down suddenly. I don't know what to do. I think back on all the stories I've heard at twelve-step meetings. I think back to what my sponsor said. Broken down, defeated, they'd all asked for help from a power that they called God. And so that's what I do—I pray . . . it is the first time I pray with sincerity. I am desperate.[4]

A psychologist who has worked in the addictions field for more than thirty years put it this way:

> Many people in recovery experience a spiritual awakening that begins with recognition of their own powerlessness. The experience is often one of struggle and conflict. They ask themselves, "Who am I? What's the purpose of my life? How can I forgive myself when I've done all

these bad things?" The questions may differ. A mother who's forty may ask, "What kind of mother was I while I was drinking?" A twenty-year-old may ask, "Who will I be?" Regardless of the questions, the place that used to be filled by chemicals must now become open to something real and meaningful.

It is no coincidence that the first of the Twelve Steps encourages people to acknowledge that they are powerless over their addiction: "We admitted that we were powerless over alcohol—that our lives had become unmanageable." Far from being an admission of defeat, the admission that they are not all-powerful is usually a prerequisite to spiritual growth.

In Shannon's words, "When I had drugs, I was on top of the world. I was it. I was almighty." It wasn't until drugs had brought her to the depths of desperation that she was able to open herself to a better way of life.

The Twelve Steps also promote spiritual growth by encouraging the development of personal values and service to others. But they are not the only route to spirituality for recovering addicts. Many develop their spirituality through active participation in religious organizations, through community service, and through the pursuit of healthy interests.

"I love my church," said one woman. "It's inclusive and welcoming and involved in a lot of community service projects. And the minister is wonderful. Her sermons always inspire me to try to be a better person."

Another woman said, "I've been volunteering at schools in a program to help kids stay off drugs. Even if I can save one kid from going through what I went through, it's worth it."

"When I was a kid, I was in a band and I'd play my guitar for hours," one man said. "When the addiction came, all that went away. Now, I've picked up a guitar and I'm playing again. It feels like a part of me that almost died is coming alive again."

Another woman has taken up gardening. "There's this little yard out back," she explained. "It was just dirt and weeds, and about three years ago I decided to plant some flowers. I'd never done anything like that before. And now it looks amazing. I love it."

Although gardening or music or volunteering might not be seen as paths to spirituality, in reality they are highly spiritual pursuits because they put people in touch with their higher selves. Or, as Jung might have put it, by nurturing the best of their inner spirit, they are quenching their spiritual thirst for wholeness.

Developing Our Own Spirituality

In our desire to support our loved ones' recovery, it can be easy to put our own needs on the back burner. It can be tempting to focus on what "they" need to do and to forget about taking care of ourselves. But recovery impacts the entire family, just as addiction did, and it is important for us to stay as healthy as possible during this time of change.

Nurturing our spiritual core is one of the best things we can do for ourselves. Focusing on the purpose of our own lives, re-examining our values, and pursuing activities that are personally meaningful can strengthen and sustain us through the inevitable ups and downs of recovery. And because spirituality by its very nature encompasses the possibility of forgiveness and redemption, developing our spirituality paves the way for healing from the wounds of addiction.

It is perhaps of interest to note that the longing for something more than the material aspects of daily life is not limited to the recovery community. There is a growing interest in spirituality throughout our society, as evidenced by the emergence of megachurches, holistic medicine, and best-selling books about the search for meaning.

It is not uncommon for recovering addicts and for families

of addicts to report that addiction brought about a surprising benefit: the development or deepening of a spiritual life. This is probably because, in times of suffering, we instinctively search for answers. In our search for answers—through reading inspirational literature, observing the world around us, and quietly listening to others—we begin to grow not only as human beings, but also as spiritual beings. In so doing, we may begin to acquire the serenity and wisdom that spirituality brings.

TIPS FOR DEALING WITH THE SOCIAL AND SPIRITUAL CHALLENGES OF EARLY RECOVERY

Supporting the Addict

1. Be willing to do legwork—find counseling if appropriate, share information about educational and work opportunities. But don't be directive.
2. Accept that your loved one has been changed by addiction. Recognize that there are many unspoken fears and unseen damages. Accept that healing will take a long time.
3. Recognize your loved one's strengths. Your loved one may have forgotten his positive qualities. Talk about past successes. Encourage him to keep trying.
4. Encourage the pursuit of activities that promote social and spiritual growth, including attendance at Twelve Step meetings.
5. Be patient. Addiction didn't wreak its damage overnight. Recovery will not happen overnight, either.

Supporting Yourself

1. Make time for yourself. Develop your hobbies and interests. Do things that bring you pleasure.
2. Strengthen your relationships with others. Nurture

your own social network and take the focus off your recovering loved one.

3. Recognize that disappointment is a part of life—and let it go. Your loved one may not have all the qualities you had hoped for. Recovery may be slow and halting. Think of the AA slogan: Progress, not perfection.

4. Cultivate gratitude. Don't focus on what you have missed out on or what is lacking. Take time to appreciate what is beautiful and good in your life.

5. Develop your spirituality. Read inspiring literature. Observe the natural world. Find a spiritual mentor, someone whose wisdom and values you admire.

CHAPTER 4

✦

SPECIAL CHALLENGES
IN EARLY RECOVERY

Life is just as it is, despite our protests. For all of us there is a constant
succession of pleasurable and painful experiences.
—SHARON SALZBURG

"If anyone had told me thirty-one years ago that my baby girl would end up like this, I don't know what I would've done," Robyn tells me. "Maybe raised her on an island somewhere. Or sent her away to a boarding school in the middle of nowhere. Anything to keep her away from bad influences."

She studies her hands, clenched in her lap, and frowns. "But maybe she would've got sick anyway."

Robyn, a widowed mother of four grown children, has invited me to her home to talk about the struggles of her youngest child, Sarah. The house is an impressive, sprawling ranch in an upscale suburb, and Robyn herself is an impeccably groomed woman with a trim figure and bobbed white hair.

"How did it all start?" I ask gently.

She draws a deep breath that is more like a sigh. "Sarah was a gifted child. Simply enchanting. She had her father wrapped around her finger." She glances at a silver-framed photograph on the mantle, in which a tall, grinning man with dark hair holds a little girl of three or four in his arms. "He died when she was eleven. A heart attack. I don't think she ever got over it."

"It must have been devastating."

"Completely. For all of us," she confirms. "I was pretty wrapped up in my own grief for a long time, and the older kids needed attention, what with preparing for college and everything. It was hard. Maybe I didn't give Sarah the attention she needed."

"You did the best you could," I offer.

She disregards my comment. "At any rate, who would have guessed the drugs that make it into suburban high schools nowadays? By the time I noticed something was wrong, she was already hooked. I got her into treatment, but things went from bad to worse. One day I found her on the patio with a knife, threatening to kill people who weren't even there." Her face is set, her jaw firm, but her eyes tear up at the memory.

"My daughter is bipolar," Robyn explains after a long moment. "She's been self-medicating for most of her life. And because of her illness, she's gone through hell."

She dabs away moisture at the corners of her eyes. "But she's doing better, for the moment, anyway. She has a good therapist, and she's been clean and sober eight months. We're what you would call cautiously optimistic. But we've learned to take it one day at a time."

Getting sober is a "one day at a time" effort for most addicts. But there are some circumstances—including co-occurring disorders, incarceration, and prostitution—that make the struggle even harder. To better understand how these issues affect the struggle for recovery, we'll begin by examining the intersection of mental health problems and addiction.

THE DOUBLE CHALLENGE
OF CO-OCCURRING DISORDERS

Approximately four million adults in the United States have both a serious mental illness and a substance use disorder—a co-occurring disorder—according to the Substance Abuse and Mental Health Services Administration's (SAMHSA) 2002 National Survey on Drug Use and Health.

Data show that 33 percent of adults with a serious mental illness abuse alcohol or other drugs, while only 8 percent of adults without serious mental illness are chemically dependent. Furthermore, almost two in three adults who abuse or are dependent on both alcohol and other drugs have a co-occurring psychiatric disorder.

The implications of these figures are significant. Coping with mental illness is in itself a major struggle that requires long-term treatment, consistent monitoring, and appropriate support. When the serious negative impact of substance abuse is complicated by the severe challenges of mental disorders, the road to recovery is likely to be long and rocky.

Which Came First?

Families of addicts are often confused about whether their loved one's irrational actions are the result of substance abuse or of some underlying psychological problem. I can remember spending a lot of time trying to figure out my daughter's erratic behavior. I feared that she was mentally ill and discussed my concerns with friends. Many of them assured me that addiction itself was the problem and that if she would only get clean, the mental health issues would go away.

But that wasn't the case. She was eventually diagnosed with depression and anxiety disorders. After that, I kept wondering if her mental disorders were the result of all the substances she had used, or if her substance abuse had been triggered by her mental disorders.

It's a question that has received a fair amount of attention in the treatment community.

The problem of co-occurring mental health disorders and substance abuse was not widely recognized until the 1980s. This may have been because chronic substance abuse can cause psychiatric symptoms and mimic psychiatric disorders. It can also lead to the development of or worsen the severity of psychiatric disorders.

The debate about which came first—the psychiatric disorder or the substance abuse—further divided opinion about how best to treat addicted individuals with symptoms of mental disorders. Clinicians who believed that substance abusers were essentially self-medicating underlying psychiatric problems emphasized the need to treat the mental disorder and minimized the need for substance abuse treatment. Clinicians who believed that psychiatric problems were caused by the substances themselves argued that the problems would disappear once abstinence was achieved.

Ongoing research has led to a better understanding of co-occurring disorders and their treatment. The National Comorbidity Survey spearheaded by Dr. Ronald Kessler in the early 1990s—the first nationally representative survey of the prevalence and correlates of psychiatric disorders—concluded that mental disorders occurred prior to the development of substance abuse in more than 85 percent of those with co-occurring disorders. In fact, the study found that the median age of onset of mental disorders was eleven, while the median age of onset for substance abuse disorders was between seventeen and twenty-one (depending on demographic variables).

Bert Pepper, M.D., a member of the SAMHSA Advisory Council, has worked extensively with young people with co-occurring disorders. In *Blamed and Ashamed,* a published report of the Federation of Families for Children's Mental Health, he wrote that "co-occurring disorders usually begin in childhood. Whatever the reasons, millions of Americans develop mental health disorders during childhood. The fact that millions go on to develop an alcohol and other drug abuse disorder some years later . . . suggests that they are self-medicating their depression, anxiety, confusion, disturbing conduct, and so on."[5]

The prevalence of co-occurring disorders has been widely observed by clinicians in the field. Dr. Patrice Muchowski, vice president of clinical services at a private treatment facility, noted in an interview, "There is a greater percentage of dual diagnosis than there used to be, probably because we're doing a better job of diagnosing it. Nearly 75 percent of our patients have a physical or mental diagnosis in addition to addiction illness, and about 25 percent have a serious mental illness."

She added, "The more serious the psychiatric illness, the greater the impact on addiction and recovery."

The Importance of Integrated Treatment
Although dual disorders encompass the full range of psychiatric disorders and substances of abuse, the four most common co-occurring psychiatric disorders are depression, anxiety, post-traumatic stress disorder (PTSD), and personality disorder. Diagnosis of mental illness is generally based on criteria established by the American Psychiatric Association, including the presence of functional impairment that substantially interferes with one or more major life activities.

Douglas Ziedonis, M.D., a contributing author of SAMHSA's Treatment Improvement Protocols (TIPS) for the treatment of substance abuse, explained in an interview, "Dual diagnosis is a simple term for a complex condition with many subtypes. If you have one mental illness, you're more likely to have another. If you abuse one substance, you're more likely to abuse another. It's all about risk. People with multiple problems have a harder time."

As one example of the challenges of treating dual disorders, Dr. Ziedonis pointed to the many medications that are helpful in stabilizing moods. "Giving a pill to an addicted individual is different from giving a pill to someone who does not have addiction illness," he observed. "If an addict is having a bad day, he might decide to take three pills. If he's having a good day, he might not take any. Compliance is always an issue."

Other factors, including the level of alcohol or illicit drugs in the system, hormonal levels, nutrition, and where an individual is in his or her life cycle can also have an impact on the diagnosis and treatment of co-occurring disorders at any given time. For example, the fluctuation of hormones associated with premenstrual syndrome (PMS) can exacerbate anxiety and depression in women, while retirement can increase the risk of depression in older people.

"Dual disorders are not a static condition, but rather a set of conditions that interact with the circumstances of an individual's life," said Dr. Ziedonis. "Treatment needs to be monitored and adjusted according to how well a patient is coping with life. We all do better or worse at different times in our lives."

Because mental health problems and substance abuse problems interact within an individual, research has consistently shown that treatment of either disorder alone is ineffective. The best hope for recovery from co-occurring mental health and substance abuse disorders comes from the integrated treatment of both conditions. This means that the patient has one medical chart that accurately reflects his or her treatment history and progress, and that treatment is provided by a team of individuals from varied clinical backgrounds who work together to develop and implement a long-term treatment strategy.

Dr. Pepper wrote in *Blamed and Ashamed* that "treatment integration is essential, because the commonest cause of mental health relapse in this population is continued use of alcohol and other drug abuse. AND, the commonest cause of relapse to the use of alcohol and other drug abuse is untreated mental health problems, such as panic-anxiety and depression."[6]

In Dr. Muchowski's experience, patients with untreated mental health issues always have a strong risk of relapse. "People are told that they will get better when they get sober," she observed. "That is not always the case. Some people get sober and things get really worse. Their psychiatric problems are no longer masked, and they are overwhelmed by enormous challenges. To support recovery, it is critical to appropriately diagnose and treat the complete range of conditions each patient is struggling with."

Finding Support in Early Recovery

Integrated treatment can be hard to find. In many communities, the mental health infrastructure is designed to treat emotional problems and substance abuse as separate issues.

For Alan, a Gulf War veteran with PTSD, the lack of integrated treatment during his early years of addiction had serious consequences. His psychiatric disorders went undiagnosed as his treatment providers focused almost exclusively on the need for abstinence. "They kept telling me my problems would go away if I stopped drinking, but every time I stopped I just felt worse," he said.

He found it impossible to work and eventually ended up homeless, panhandling during the day and drinking himself into oblivion at night. He rejected offers of help from his distraught family. "I didn't think I deserved it, and besides, I didn't want to get sober," he explained.

One day, he got into a fight with another alcoholic and was seriously injured. In the hospital, he received a visit from a social worker who told him about a new mental health program in the city. "That program saved my life," Alan said. "I found out what was wrong with me. It wasn't just the booze. It was something in my head that had to get fixed. There were a lot of guys out there just like me, and they were getting better. I figured if they could do it, I could, too."

Thanks to support from an integrated treatment program and active participation in AA, Alan is on the road to recovery.

Ramona's mother, Pat, was not so fortunate.

Depression and the Elderly

"My mother was always a drinker," Ramona recalled, "but after she retired, she got worse. You just didn't call after three in the afternoon. She'd start crying and complain that she was lonely. She had six kids and a bunch of grandkids, and they didn't come around that much. I left my kids overnight with her once, and the next day they told me she'd fallen asleep on the couch. They couldn't wake her up so they put themselves to bed. After that, we'd do Saturday mornings with Grandma. Mornings she was fine."

At the age of seventy-two, Pat checked herself into rehab. "They called her 'granny in the detox,'" Ramona said. "She did twenty-eight days and never touched a drop again."

The family was thrilled that Pat wasn't drinking anymore—except for her sister, who complained, "Now who am I going to have my five o'clock highball with?"

"My mother's physical health improved," said Ramona, "and we were glad she wasn't drinking and driving. But she seemed depressed, more subdued. She didn't dance around anymore. After a few drinks, she used to like to put on music and do silly little dances. We missed her sense of frivolousness, her sense of fun. I don't think being sober made her happier. I think taking the alcohol away made her see what her life had become."

Pat never went to AA—saying she wasn't going to talk about her problems with a bunch of strangers—and she never got counseling for her depression. Ramona said, "Her generation didn't talk about their problems. But maybe with more intervention, some therapy, she might have found happiness."

Pat was like many older people who suffer from depression and addiction—often to alcohol or prescription drugs. With the right mental health support, they can learn to create a more satisfying way of life. But getting appropriate services for seniors—as well as for their younger counterparts with dual disorders—can present an ongoing challenge in a mental health system that is too often mired in bureaucracy and is slow to change.

During early recovery, family members and their loved ones may need to be vocal and persistent in their efforts to obtain support for the dual challenges of addiction and psychiatric disorders.

THE PERSISTENT HANDICAP OF A CRIMINAL RECORD

Addiction is the only illness that I am aware of that carries a penalty of jail or imprisonment. I am not talking about crimes committed while under the influence of substances, or the crimes of growing, producing, or distributing illicit substances. Rather, I am referring specifically to the possession and use of illicit substances, symptoms of the disease of addiction that are routinely penalized by incarceration.

Both the American Medical Association and the American Psychiatric Association have recognized addiction as a disease since the mid-1960s. Compulsive, uncontrollable drug seeking and use are primary characteristics of the disease. Yet, because drugs of abuse (other than alcohol and nicotine) are illegal or tightly controlled substances, the criminal justice system today exerts considerable power over the lives of millions of addicted individuals.

The intersection of the law and addiction illness is, at best, an uneasy one. On one hand, coming up against the iron fist of the law is sometimes a wake-up call, a hard encounter with tough consequences that can sometimes influence addicts to get serious about recovery. On the other hand, far too many addicted individuals experience the criminal justice system as a punitive form of intervention that ultimately prolongs addiction and makes recovery harder.

Ray, who got clean eight years ago when he was forty-five, described how incarceration impacted his addiction. "I had a long-term relationship with the criminal justice system. When I think about paroles and probations and incarcerations, a lot of the time

I was running from legal issues," he reflected. "A lot of times I had warrants, and once the warrants came out, once the probation violations came out, once I was out on bail, it was full speed ahead with anything I could get my hands on."

He explained, "If you put all my time together that I accumulated in prison, it's probably around fifteen years. There were times when I'd go to jail and remain relatively clean and sober. Three years—thirty-five months and ten days—was the longest straight that I did, but the moment I walked out the door, I was headed to get high in some shape or form. In a lot of ways, I confused myself into thinking I deserved it. Regardless of what anybody says, initially, using is very rewarding. I couldn't see that I was going to end up worse in a relatively short time."

Fifteen years of incarceration had given Ray little insight into his addiction and no tools for maintaining sobriety. Worse, being behind bars had not prepared him for reentry into society. Unable to find work or housing, unskilled in building relationships, and bearing the dual stigmas of addiction and incarceration, his multiple relapses and rearrests were almost inevitable. His story is all too common.

More Jails, Less Treatment

The nation's mental health treatment system has been drastically downsized since the 1950s, when there were approximately 559,000 public mental health hospital beds. In 2001 there were only 60,000—almost half a million fewer beds! Yet during the same time period, the nation's population rose by one million people. What has happened to people in need of mental health treatment, including substance abusers? Many of them are behind bars.

From the 1970s to the new millennium, the number of people in correctional institutions rose from around 300,000 to more than two million. Although the United States has only 5 percent of the world's population, it has 25 percent of the world's prisoners. An estimated 75 percent of all prisoners are chemically addicted, and approximately 16 percent have a serious mental illness. Furthermore, about three-quarters of drug offenders in state prisons have been convicted only of drug crimes, with no convictions for violence or high-level drug activity.

Rounding out this disturbing picture is the fact that two-thirds of released prisoners are eventually rearrested, and 40 percent return to incarceration within three years.

During one of my many trips to court with my daughter—whose arrest record includes possession of heroin and marijuana, prostitution, driving under the influence of alcohol, and warrants for failure to appear in court—I got a glimpse into why recidivism rates are so high for drug offenders. A stout white-haired lawyer in a black suit was standing across from me in the hallway. He was talking to his client, a slender young Hispanic man who was charged with cocaine possession.

"They're offering you six months probation instead of jail," he said. "You'll have to pay sixty-five dollars a month and take random drug tests. If even one of them comes back positive for anything, including marijuana, you're going to jail for two years. No one can get you out of that. Do you understand?"

The young man nodded.

"Do you think you can do it?"

He nodded again. "Yes. I can do that. I don't want to go to jail." His voice rose a little, probably from anxiety.

The lawyer gave him an encouraging pat on the back, but I couldn't help feeling uneasy as I watched them return to the courtroom. I understood why the young man had chosen probation over an immediate jail sentence. I believed that he sincerely intended to abstain from substances for the duration of his probation. And he may have done so—I have no way of knowing what ultimately happened to him. What I do know is that sending an addicted individual out into the world with no treatment program and no support system in place is likely to result in failure. That is because *the compulsion to use despite negative consequences* is a defining characteristic of addiction illness.

If, like so many drug offenders, the young man violated his probation and wound up behind bars, our society's policy of treating addiction as a crime rather than an illness will have made his future attempts at recovery all the more challenging. He will face discrimination in his search for employment and housing, and he will carry the damaging effects of "prison culture" for years to come.

The War on Drugs, or Legally Sanctioned Discrimination

Addiction is highly stigmatized in our society, despite widespread recognition that addiction is an illness. People with addiction illness are routinely stereotyped as weak, immoral, and untrustworthy. It is not hard to see why this perception exists, especially for those of us who have witnessed firsthand the moral deterioration that generally accompanies addiction. Certainly, few people—if any—would want to have an active addict as a neighbor, tenant, or employee. Even parents who love their children unconditionally must sometimes make the excruciating decision to bar their addicted children from their homes.

Unfortunately, the negative behaviors associated with addiction loom so large in the public mind that even people with successful, long-term recoveries are stigmatized in a way that individuals with other mental or physical disorders are not. A history of addiction can diminish an individual's ability to become integrated into society (both because of damaged self-esteem and because of negative response from others) and—especially for those whose addiction has resulted in a criminal record—severely limit housing, education, and employment opportunities.

The wide availability of criminal background checks has resulted in legally sanctioned discrimination against millions of Americans with addiction disorders. Under the guise of protecting public safety and being "tough on drugs," our society routinely denies people in recovery from these illnesses many of the privileges and protections that most of us take for granted. Landlords can decline to rent to them. Access to student loans can be denied. Prospective employers can choose not to "risk" hiring someone with a known history of addiction.

All of this, of course, is done in the name of security—but it is a false sense of security at best. Just as many of us manage to avoid getting a speeding ticket when we're driving too fast, many substance abusers manage to avoid getting arrested and therefore have no criminal record. Criminal background checks are useful only for screening out those who have been caught.

Furthermore, background checks enable employers and others to scrutinize only specific types of past undesirable behavior. Dishonesty, incompetence, pettiness, cruelty, and laziness are just a few of a whole host of human flaws and foibles that cannot be detected by background checks. Criminal records provide a glimpse into only one aspect of a person's past, while shedding no light on a person's positive qualities.

Another weakness of background checks is the fact that past behavior—whether blemished or blemish-free—is not necessarily a predictor of future behavior. People can and do change all the time, sometimes for the better, sometimes for the worse. In reality, there is simply no guarantee that any tenant, student, or employee—regardless of past problems or mistakes—will live up to anyone's expectations.

Rather than criminalizing addiction and then broadly releasing those criminal records—something our society would find unacceptable for people with a history of bipolar disorder, diabetes, or other chronic medical conditions—government agencies that want to help organizations achieve drug-free environments can do so more effectively by implementing drug-testing policies. That would enable employers and others to evaluate people based on current behavior. At the same time, it would remove the crippling penalties our laws currently impose on individuals who are recovering from addiction illness.

The Trauma of Prison Culture

Unfortunately, the damage done by criminalizing addiction is not limited to the discrimination faced by those with a criminal record. Time spent behind bars can result in long-lasting psychological trauma.

Jails and prisons are meant to be a form of punishment. That is their purpose. Although public safety and rehabilitation also factor into the rationale for imprisonment, the primary function of jails and prisons is to punish. Consequently, the prison environment is harsh.

Life behind bars strips individuals of their freedom, privacy, and individuality. Prisoners are subjected to the use of force and restraint, humiliating searches, arbitrary harassment, and crowded and dehumanizing living conditions. They face threats from guards and other inmates and can end up in isolation units (which can produce psychosis) for minor infractions of rules.

For the mentally ill (keep in mind that nearly two in three substance abusers have a serious mental illness), imprisonment is even more damaging. They are victims of abuse and attacks from other inmates. They are likely to be shunned and called derogatory names. Many either withdraw into their cells or act out, which lands them in solitary confinement. Either way, social and sensory deprivation makes their problems worse.

The experience of having a loved one incarcerated is also apt to be painful for family members. One father recalled, "The first time I saw my daughter enter the courtroom in handcuffs and with shackles on her legs, my heart broke. She was my little girl." Another man remembered that, while visiting his wife in prison, where she was serving a six-month sentence for forging prescriptions, "All I could think about was how fragile she looked, how she didn't belong there, and how I had failed to protect her."

The experience is even harder for addicts with children at home. One woman recalled her husband's two years of incarceration for probation violations as "a nightmare." She said, "Our kids cried a lot, maybe because I was so stressed out, and every time we visited him in prison, they would act up afterward. I think they hated seeing their father like that."

I remember crying myself to sleep almost every night during the ten days of my own daughter's incarceration for failing to pay court fines. I had chosen not to rescue her, but that did not prevent me from being brokenhearted over her situation. Unfortunately, it also did not prevent her from returning to substance abuse when she was released.

How much better would it have been, I have often wondered, if instead of sending her to prison, the courts had sent her to a treatment facility where she could have begun to get help for her mental and substance abuse disorders?

Similar questions are being raised across the country as the debate about whether to punish substance abusers or provide treatment for them gathers momentum.

Changing the System

The United States spends more than $60 billion a year on prisons to lock up more than 2.2 million people—more than any other postindustrial nation. The high rate of recidivism among drug offenders and the skyrocketing costs of prisons are beginning to bring about changes in the way the criminal justice system deals with addicted individuals.

Some states—recognizing that reintegration into society is crucial for long-term recovery from addiction illness—are reexamining their criminal background check laws with an eye to removing barriers to housing, education, and employment.

In addition, treatment programs are increasingly being integrated into sentences, both during and after incarceration. The Delaware Department of Correction, for example, has introduced a treatment program for inmates, with continued treatment in a follow-up work-release program. A study showed that participants were 70 percent less likely than nonparticipants to relapse to drug use or be rearrested.

In 2004, the state of Illinois launched the Sheridan National Model Drug Prison and Reentry Program—the nation's first prison designed exclusively for drug offenders. This cutting-edge program immerses every inmate—1,300 at any given time—into a therapeutic community that includes intensive substance abuse treatment, counseling, mental health services, and job preparedness training. Early results indicate that the program is living up to its goal of reducing recidivism rates and helping former inmates achieve stable, productive lives.

Drug courts are also being established in some cities and have the authority to mandate treatment as an alternative to incarceration, monitor progress in treatment, and arrange for additional services. Texas, for example, has established about eighty problem-solving courts across the state to keep people with minor drug offenses out of jail and to get them into treatment. One of them, the Dallas Initiative for Diversion and Expedited Rehabilitation and Treatment (DIVERT) court, has been so successful that the state is examining ways to expand the program beyond first-time offenders.

Judge John Creuzot, who runs the DIVERT court, has commented on the philosophical differences between his court and more punitive approaches to substance abuse. For example, when a young woman had a positive drug test while on probation, he sent her to forty-five days of intensive inpatient treatment instead of sending her to jail.

"A person who relapses on drugs needs further treatment," he stated in a National Public Radio interview. "Our responses are research-driven."

In fact, two studies by Southern Methodist University showed that the DIVERT court has cut the recidivism rate by 68 percent over traditional Texas courts and that for every dollar spent on the court, nine dollars have been saved in additional criminal justice costs.

The most important savings, however, come in terms of human lives.

Although traditional punitive approaches to addiction have undoubtedly served as an important wake-up call for some people, high recidivism rates among addicts demonstrate that a "stop using or go to jail" approach generally does not work. Addicts who get caught up in the revolving door of incarceration and recidivism have a hard time reintegrating into society—something they must do to maintain sobriety.

As the criminal justice system begins to reexamine its approach to substance abuse, there are encouraging signs that change is happening, however slowly. In the meantime, the trauma and lasting stigma of incarceration continue to present significant challenges for many people seeking recovery.

SEX AND DRUGS AND LONG-TERM TRAUMA

Steve and Terri were disgusted by their daughter's lifestyle. At twenty-four, she was addicted to crystal meth and turning tricks to pay for her drugs.

"I was furious with her," Terri said. "We didn't raise her that way. It was like she turned her back on every value we ever taught her."

Steve added, "What made me even madder was the way she made her mother suffer. Terri worried herself sick, crying, blaming herself, not eating, not sleeping. It was horrible."

"I spent a lot of time asking myself, *Why?*" Terri recalled. "How does a nice, middle-class girl from a good family end up walking the streets?"

It's a painful question that many families of addicted women have had to grapple with. On top of that, there's another, tougher question that demands our attention: How does prostitution impact recovery?

It is very common for women who become addicted to drugs—other than alcohol, which is cheap and readily available—to turn to prostitution to support their habit. Most of them say, "It just kind of happened."

Jane, Steve and Terri's daughter, recalled that one day she was desperate for drugs, and when a man gave her a certain "look," she asked herself, *Why not?*

"I never saw myself going that route," she said. "I thought I was smarter than that. But when you're strung out, nothing else matters." On a typical day she'd get four or five "dates"—most of them involving oral sex—and make more than a hundred dollars. Of course, most of it went to drugs. Before long, her boyfriend was counting on the money, too. He'd tell her to "go out and make some money," and when she came home, they'd celebrate by getting high.

"I kept telling myself it was just a job. I mean, women have sex with guys they don't like all the time, for security or to be popular or whatever," Jane reasoned. "But deep down I hated it and I hated myself. The more I did it, the more I had to use. And the more I used, the more I had to do it. I couldn't see any way out."

Almost without knowing it, Jane had joined one of the most stigmatized segments of our society: addicted prostitutes.

A Vicious Cycle

Despite the proliferation of pornography in our society and the entertainment industry's glamorization of recreational sex, addicted streetwalkers are often seen as the lowest of the low. Murderers, muggers, and sociopaths of every stripe seek them out as easy targets. Some cops demand sexual favors in return for not arresting them. And pimps and boyfriends sell them as casually as they would an inanimate object.

Women in prostitution cope with extraordinary levels of violence, harassment, and dehumanization every day. As a result, they have high rates of PTSD as well as anxiety disorders, mood disorders, personality disorders, and frequent thoughts of suicide. Prostitution, trauma, and substances overlap as a complex set of issues that must all be addressed before recovery can be sustained.

One counselor who works extensively with women in prostitution observed, "Many of them have a profound sense of loss—loss of family, friends, credibility, and self-respect. They're also deeply lonely. Even though they know each other, they don't like each other very much. They don't know how to connect with other women." Instead, she said, they think of their pimps and johns as "friends" and hang on to customer phone numbers as a kind of insurance policy.

Research shows that close to 90 percent of women involved in prostitution want to leave the lifestyle. But getting out can be extremely difficult. For one thing, even entry-level jobs can be hard to come by for women with few job skills and little education. Despite the tremendous physical and psychological toll of prostitution, it has economic credibility for women with limited options. Furthermore, many women in prostitution come to rely on the companionship of the very men who exploit them. As social outcasts, they nevertheless have the normal human longing to belong somewhere.

Most significantly, their use of substances keeps them tethered to prostitution in a dark cycle of mutual reinforcement. Prostitution creates pain, for which they turn to substances, for which they turn to prostitution, and on it goes.

Jane, who recently celebrated her first year of recovery, said that she has had a hard time accepting her past. "I look back on myself and I still feel ashamed, even though I know it was the drugs that made me do it," she said. "I think it'll take a long time for those feelings to go away."

"We're proud of what our daughter has accomplished, but it took a lot of counseling before we began to accept prostitution as part of the disease of addiction," Steve admitted. "We kept thinking of it as a separate thing, but it's all part of the same sad package."

FAMILY SUPPORT

Mental illness, incarceration, and prostitution make the road to recovery especially challenging for many addicts. These complex issues present significant challenges for the people who love them, as well.

During the years of active addiction, we have clung to the hope that abstinence will solve our loved one's problems. But many of us find that they face ongoing difficulties, some of which were masked by substances and others that are consequences of addiction. Moodiness, irritability, and other difficult behaviors may continue well after a prolonged period of abstinence has been achieved. Our loved ones may be unable—for a while, at least—to manage their lives without substantial support. They may reveal themselves to be far different from the person we had hoped they would be.

As family members, our challenge is to offer support to an extent that is appropriate while maintaining an attitude of healthy detachment. We can begin to do this by cultivating an attitude of acceptance. By accepting the reality of what has happened and of where our loved ones are at this moment in time, we are free to let go of the past and focus instead on the challenges and opportunities of the present.

Acceptance also frees us of our illusions about who our loved ones should be and allows us to discover instead who they really are. What do they want out of life, where do they see themselves going, and to what extent do they want our help in getting there?

It is fine and even necessary in some cases for family members to take the lead in accessing mental health and other services. By doing some of the legwork, we can help our loved ones get the treatment they need. It is important, however, to avoid sending the message that we don't think they can handle things on their own or that we want to control their lives.

Practical support can be valuable—but emotional support founded on acceptance and respect is often even more helpful.

Furthermore, in our desire to be supportive, it is important not to abandon one of the primary tools for coping with addiction: detachment. Detachment is just as important during the process of recovery as it was during active addiction.

Detachment does not mean that we're indifferent to or alienated from our loved ones. It means that we allow them to live their lives to the best of their ability and that we take responsibility for living our own lives to the best of our ability. In the words of one counselor, we "don't internalize their pain."

Detachment does not come easily for most of us, especially when someone we love is struggling. But it is an attitude worth striving for. Healthy detachment allows us to be supportive without being intrusive. It enables us to create respectful relationships that support recovery—our loved one's and our own. And it gives us the freedom to make the most of our own lives.

TIPS FOR DEALING WITH THE SPECIAL CHALLENGES OF EARLY RECOVERY

Supporting the Addict

1. Get educated about dual disorders. Understanding the interplay of psychiatric disorders and addiction enables you to be more realistic in your expectations, and therefore more helpful.

2. Listen. Let go of paying attention to what you expect to hear and listen to what your loved one tells you. Listening more and talking less are the foundations of healthy communication.

3. Encourage your loved one to get professional help. Mental illness and trauma don't go away on their own. The right treatment can greatly improve the quality of your loved one's life.

4. Be willing to do the legwork. Accessing mental health services can be frustrating and full of obstacles. Find appropriate services, share information with your loved one, and be willing to provide rides or whatever you can to facilitate treatment.

5. Cultivate a positive attitude. Your loved one is full of self-doubt. Be positive—in a realistic way. Instead of saying, "I'm afraid you won't make it," say, "I have confidence in you. I know you can do it." A positive attitude nurtures hope, a necessary piece of the process of change.

Supporting Yourself

1. Work through your grief. Addiction is a series of losses, especially the loss of the way you dreamed life would be. Acknowledge your grief so you can move on.

2. Let go of guilt. You may feel that you failed your loved one in some significant way. Whatever your mistakes, you did not cause the addiction or the resulting problems. Guilt is a self-focused emotion that damages relationships. Make your amends and let it go.

3. Let go of expectations. You may have harbored expectations about who your loved one would become once recovery took hold. This only sets you up for disappointment. Let your loved one's life unfold along his chosen path.

4. Cultivate acceptance. This does not mean giving up or giving in. It does not signal defeat. Acceptance is the courage to let go of illusion and come face to face with what is.

5. Take care of your own life. Fixing someone else's problems can seem more compelling than addressing your own issues. But keeping the focus on yourself is the only way to live fully and to celebrate the distinctly individual person that is you.

CHAPTER 5

SLIPS, RELAPSES, AND OTHER BUMPS IN THE ROAD

Be not angry that you cannot make others as you wish them to be,
since you cannot make yourself as you wish to be.
—THOMAS À KEMPIS

John, a broadly built man with a hangdog face and threads of gray in his dark hair, takes a deep breath before starting to speak. He has been attending the Tuesday night support group for more than three years, and the people seated around the table are like family.

Together they have shared the heartache of loving an addict and celebrated their hard-earned successes: being detached (sometimes), minding their own business (most of the time), and—to the best of their ability—replacing fear with faith and despair with hope. They have exchanged tales that made them laugh or cry, and hugged close to their hearts the occasional, heartening stories of a loved one's recovery. Those are the stories that sustain them through the bad times, reminding them that no case is hopeless and that recovery can happen when we least expect it.

John's daughter Lilly is a case in point. Addicted to alcohol, meth, and other drugs for ten years, she has miraculously turned her life around. She is living in another state, is sharing an apartment with a woman in recovery, and has been working in a bakery for the past nine months. She seems positive and cheerful for the first time in many years. She's even started a relationship with a man she met at an AA meeting. John and his wife have begun to hope that the worst is behind them, and that their beloved thirty-three-year-old daughter is on her way to a stable and happy life.

"We got a call last night," he tells the group. The tremor in his voice leaves no doubt that the call was not a good one. "She told us she relapsed. She's been using for about a month. She lost her job and can't pay the rent."

There are murmurs of sympathy around the table. Some people give him looks of concern. Others bow their heads. He swallows hard a couple of times. "She was crying. She asked if we'd help her out until she gets back on her feet."

His wife reaches over and covers his hand with her own. Someone pushes a box of tissues toward them. "I told her we can't do it. Not anymore." The raggedness in his voice betrays the difficulty of the decision. "She has to get back into treatment. That's her only option. She knows. She agreed."

His wife pulls a tissue from the box and wipes her own eyes.

"She's supposed to make some calls today, try to get in someplace." He clenches his wife's hand and stares hard at some point only he can see. "I can't believe it's starting all over again."

There's a silence while the group digests the news. Even though they know that relapse happens, that it's part of the process, it's like a physical blow. She had been doing so well. She was on the right track. And now . . .

John shakes his head. The lines in his face have visibly deepened. After a moment, he voices the question that's in everyone's mind: "I just can't stop asking myself, *Why? Why?*"

RELAPSE AND THE STAGES OF CHANGE

Of all the suffering created by addiction, perhaps nothing causes families more pain than relapse.

During the years of active addiction, we find ways to cope with symptoms of the disease. We learn that our loved one can't be trusted and won't be responsible. We learn to establish boundaries and detach from his problems. And we learn that our peace of mind depends not on what *he* does but on what *we* do.

Still, when recovery begins, many of those lessons go out the window. Our loved one shows signs of growth and responsibility, so we begin to trust. She pursues healthy activities, so we begin to rebuild connections. She establishes a record of sobriety, so we begin to believe the worst is over.

All of this is normal and natural—and it sets us up for a big fall when a relapse occurs.

"Relapse can be devastating for the family and the user," noted one therapist. "It's helpful if families can recognize that it's probably going to happen and to roll with it. But that's easier said than done."

"Families should be hopeful if someone is getting sober," advised a recovering alcoholic, "but they shouldn't get their hopes up too high. Because, you know, it can all change in a minute."

Setbacks can happen with recovery from any illness. Addiction is no different. But relapse can feel different because, along with renewed concerns for our loved one's health and well-being, relapse imposes an added layer of emotional distress. We've let our guard down, welcomed the prodigal into our hearts—and been robbed, lied to, or manipulated in return. There's a sense of betrayal, as if we've somehow had the wool pulled over our eyes. It's depressing. And it hurts.

But it doesn't have to be that way. Understanding relapse as part of a process can help us get a better perspective. In reality, when any of us attempts to make a significant personal change—such as improving our health habits, building more satisfying relationships, or doing a better job of managing our finances—it's almost inevitable that we'll return to our old familiar behaviors at least a few times before we succeed.

In fact, relapse is so common to the human experience that it is an integral part of the stages of change, a model of behavior developed by American psychologists James Prochaska and Carlo DiClemente. This widely accepted model states that behavioral changes rarely occur spontaneously. Rather, they are most often the result of a six-stage process: precontemplation, contemplation, preparation, action, maintenance, and termination.

Precontemplation is a condition of unawareness in which we don't recognize a need for change, or we believe that change is not possible. Contemplation is a time of awakening, when we see a need for change but are not ready to do anything about it. Preparation, the next stage, brings a growing sense of self-efficacy as we develop a plan of action. During the action stage, we take the necessary steps to bring about the desired change before moving on to maintenance. In this stage, we keep an eye on things and make adjustments as needed to make the change permanent. Stage six, termination, is reached when the change has become so ingrained that there is no longer any risk that the former behavior will reappear. Some psychologists doubt that termination is ever fully achieved, noting that there is always a possibility for past behaviors to return.

Most people with long-term recovery recognize this risk. That is why, even after ten years or more of sobriety, many have a maintenance program that includes at least one Twelve Step meeting a week or some other tool to keep them on track.

Relapse Is Part of the Process

Significantly, the stages of change model asserts that we seldom progress smoothly from one stage to the next, like someone climbing methodically up a flight of stairs. Instead, we cycle through the various stages many times, sometimes moving up, sometimes slipping down, until the desired behavioral change is finally achieved. Furthermore, when we move backward, we can find ourselves at any of the preceding stages of change—the one right below us or all the way back at precontemplation, telling ourselves yet again that change is neither desirable nor possible.

Consider a friend of mine who has struggled with her weight for years. There are times when she eats well and exercises regularly. During those periods, she brims with confidence, saying such things as, "I feel so much better about myself now. My whole attitude is different. I love being healthy." Then, there are times when she is still struggling to maintain healthy habits but has given in to a craving for chocolate cake and skipped exercising for a few days. "I'm losing control," she'll say, "and I've got to get to the gym tomorrow."

Occasionally, she gives up completely. In those moments she is apt to exclaim, "What's the point? I've always been heavy and I've accepted the fact. That's who I am, and there's nothing I can do about it."

Most of us have gone through similar experiences, if not with our weight, then with an unfulfilling job, a difficult relationship, or some other significant aspect of our lives. After a period of unawareness or indecision, we finally move ahead, feel we are making progress, and then *wham!* For reasons that may be hard to define, we find ourselves right back where we started, or at least further back than we want to be.

Recovering from addiction follows the same type of self-talk, significantly complicated by chemical changes within the brain. Sometimes our loved ones move forward, and sometimes they slip back. It's a normal part of the process of change. However, to be able to sustain their recovery, all addicts must learn how to avoid relapses. Without that know-how, they may enter a disheartening cycle of alternating abstinence and using, living their lives like hamsters on a wheel. Studies have shown, for example, that heroin addicts typically go through as many as ten to twenty-five treatment programs before achieving recovery—an emotional roller coaster for addicts and for the people who love them.

To get off the roller coaster and into sustained recovery, our loved one must be able to recognize and avoid common relapse triggers; to get appropriate support if a relapse seems imminent; and to prevent a slip—a brief return to addictive thinking or behaviors—from turning into a full-blown relapse.

Common Relapse Triggers
Relapse is closely linked to association. Our brains are wired to associate certain cues with specific responses: If we're in danger, we run or fight back; if we're hungry or thirsty, we head to the kitchen (or the next best source of food or drink). When we repeatedly respond in identical ways to specific cues, neurological pathways are formed in our brains. Every time we encounter those cues—which can be emotions, activities, people, places, or things—our well-worn pathways get activated. Neurons flood the pathways, urging us to respond exactly as we have in the past.

The process is instantaneous and subconscious. We don't even think about it. Thus, we become creatures of habit, automatically reaching for a bag of chips when we watch our favorite television show, automatically withdrawing into sulky silence when our spouse comes home late.

With chemical addiction, anything associated with using is a potential trigger for relapse. It often begins with emotions. "Relapse doesn't just happen out of nowhere," noted a clinician who has worked in a publicly funded treatment facility for many years. "There is a way of thinking that precedes the decision to pick up, a kind of emotional relapse that occurs before the actual physical relapse happens."

For example, when our loved one can't make a decision, has intense feelings of being up or down, or is depressed, anxious, negative, or distracted, it may be a sign that he's right at the door of picking up again. (A common acronym for relapse triggers is HALT: hungry, angry, lonely, and tired.) Boredom is also a common prelude to relapse because the addicted brain is ill-equipped for coping with uncomfortable feelings. In fact, anything that causes distress—not getting enough sleep, poor nutrition, not getting a job or getting a job, starting or ending a relationship, having an argument, being criticized, or even something as mundane as missing a bus or misplacing a key—has the potential to trigger a relapse because the brain has been conditioned to associate chemicals with relief from stress.

Ironically, happy feelings can be triggers for the same reason—the brain associates feelings of euphoria with substances. It says to the addict, "You feel good now. You'll feel even better with a chemical fix."

But emotional ups and downs are only part of the story. Anything associated with using can trigger intense cravings and lead to a relapse. For example, it is widely recognized that returning to the old neighborhood after treatment presents significant challenges for people in early recovery. The same is true for people recently released from incarceration. On the surface, this may not make sense. After all, addicts have received valuable education and support during treatment as well as tools for maintaining sobriety. Those who were incarcerated have sometimes received similar information and have also experienced serious negative consequences of their addiction.

No matter how ingrained the lessons resulting from treatment or incarceration, however, addicts cannot erase the automatic process of association. Encountering using buddies, being in places where they bought or used drugs, seeing their old dealers or liquor store clerks—even witnessing a scene that resembles past experiences are all powerful reminders of the pleasurable aspects of getting high. So are more ordinary, less obvious events.

One young woman reported that the sight of spoons was a trigger because spoons had been part of the process of preparing her drugs. Matchbooks had a similar effect on another woman.

A young man said that being in a bathroom made him think about using because that was where he had always gone to shoot up. For another, it was being in the front passenger seat of a car.

Triggers abound for the newly recovering addict, creating strong cravings for the substances that are being withheld. Given enough time, the power of triggers subsides. The brain learns to associate old cues with new responses. But learning to replace negative responses with positive ones can be an arduous process.

The Slippery Slope of Self-deception

Whatever their triggers, addicts are especially vulnerable to them in early recovery. They simply have not had enough time for their old neurological response pathways to be rerouted into healthier patterns, and their skills for coping with cravings are most likely shaky.

Another period of high vulnerability occurs a few months into recovery, when confidence is high. Addicts may begin to believe that they have kicked their habit, and they may be tempted to let their guard down. They may attend fewer Twelve Step meetings or stop going altogether. They may blow off counseling sessions or stop checking in with their sponsor. They may put themselves in risky situations with the mistaken belief that they can "handle" them.

Seth, my daughter's high school sweetheart, had moved to another state and been clean nine months when he returned to take care of some outstanding warrants. He was working and wanted to buy a car but needed to clear his record to renew his license. After paying his fines, he was left with almost a thousand dollars. He and my daughter spent a day together (she was on methadone at the time), and then he returned home. He promptly relapsed. He lost his job and went through all his money without getting a car.

Later, when he was back on track, I asked him what had led to the relapse. "I think it was just having all that money in my pocket," he said. Maybe. But it may have had a lot to do with his high level of confidence and being in the old neighborhood where he and my daughter had used so many drugs together. The combination of letting his guard down and being bombarded with triggers may have been too much for him.

A young woman who relapsed eight months into her recovery from crack cocaine recalled that she "ended up drinking in a bar one night. I thought I could handle it because I didn't really like alcohol." She told herself that having a drink wasn't a relapse because alcohol was not her drug of choice. Someone at the bar was selling drugs, and before long, she was using crack again.

Another woman had been heroin-free for nearly a year when she returned home and started hanging out with her old friends. Within a month, she was using cocaine on a regular basis. She, too, convinced herself that she hadn't relapsed because she hadn't reverted to her primary addiction. But before long, she was back on heroin.

What did these two women have in common? Their successful recovery was undermined by self-deception. They not only convinced themselves that they weren't vulnerable to relapse, but they also fooled themselves into believing that they could safely use an addictive chemical as long as it wasn't their substance of choice. What began as a relapse into denial quickly blossomed into a full-blown physical relapse.

There's an old AA slogan that says, "One drink is too many, and a thousand is never enough." It points to the inability of people with addictions to moderate their use of addictive substances. One drink, hit, or pill leads to another, and then another, and then a slippery slide down the precipitous slope. That is why, for most people with addictions, abstinence from all mood-altering chemicals is the absolute foundation of recovery.

However, it is possible to teeter on the brink of the relapse slope without toppling over. Slipping up and taking a drink or a fix can be just a momentary lapse. It all depends on what happens next.

How Slips Become Relapses

If we compare being in recovery to being on a diet, a slip is like eating a hot fudge sundae after a week of healthy eating. If the dieter immediately goes back to making healthy choices, not much harm will have been done. Progress may have been slowed a little bit, but some valuable lessons may have also been gained. The dieter may have learned to avoid a certain place or situation, or the slip may have led to better self-knowledge. In other words, a slip can be an opportunity for personal growth.

Recognizing that we are not invincible can strengthen our resolve and make us more alert to potential pitfalls.

On the other hand, a slip can in itself be a powerful relapse trigger. The nature of addiction is that having a little bit never satisfies. It simply stimulates cravings for more. This is as true for addictions to food, tobacco, and certain behaviors (such as sex addiction) as it is for addictions to mood-altering chemicals. (The people who created that old potato chip commercial "Bet you can't eat just one!" knew what they were talking about.) That is why abstinence is so fundamental to recovery. People with addiction illness find it very hard to stop once they start.

Furthermore, slips can produce a barrage of negative emotions that pave the way for a complete relapse. The addict who slips, like the dieter who slips, might begin to think, *I'm a failure. I'm a loser. I might as well give up and eat/drink/use as much as I want.* Negative self-talk (or "stinking thinking") can lead to a feeling of hopelessness, which undermines the motivation to change.

"Addicts tend to beat themselves up for not being perfect," noted one counselor. "Where you or I might say, 'Oh, that didn't work out very well. I'd better try something different,' an addict is likely to say, 'I'm stupid. I can't do anything right. I should stop trying.' They think of themselves as a bad person, rather than as a good person who made a bad choice."

Slips bring out the sense of shame that is never far beneath the surface of addicts in early recovery. This, along with feelings of failure and hopelessness, can become almost unbearable for people whose coping skills are shaky at best. Unless they have a strong support system to help them get back on track, it is a very small leap for a slip to become a full-scale relapse into the comforting oblivion of substances.

THE FAMILY'S DILEMMA

People who love an addict can usually recognize when a return to drinking or drugging is imminent or under way. The old addict behaviors begin to emerge, such as evasiveness, defensiveness, isolating, and lying. Although everyone sees the change in the addict, anyone who raises the possibility of relapse is likely to be met with angry denial.

The whole question of relapse places the family in a painfully difficult position. On one hand, we don't want to ignore the situation and retreat into our own state of denial. On the other hand, we don't want to take on the role of watchdog and monitor the addict's every move. One woman recalled, for example, how her suspicious husband followed her around during her first months of recovery. "Even when I was in the shower, he'd knock on the door and ask, 'Are you all right?' He wasn't being supportive. He was controlling."

And even if our fears are justified and our loved one has slipped or relapsed, what can we do? It is not our job to manage our loved one's recovery—even if we could.

Mary faced this heart-wrenching situation when her husband came home after six months in a recovery house. She was cautiously optimistic that things would be better. She was thrilled to see him going to AA meetings every night and twice a day on weekends. But after two or three months, she noticed disturbing changes in his behavior.

At first, he was moody and irritable. "I know early recovery's hard, and I didn't expect him to be Mr. Cheerful all the time," she said. "But the mood swings were pretty bad." She asked if anything was wrong, but he shrugged her off. When she suggested that he should call his sponsor or try getting to extra meetings, he told her to mind her own business.

"He started coming home from his meetings later and later without really explaining why," Mary continued. "And he missed work because he couldn't get up in the morning. I knew what was happening, but it took me a while to confront him."

When she did, her husband vehemently denied that anything was wrong. "The way he reacted convinced me more than anything that he was using," Mary said. "It was just like the old days. He was furious and said that everything was my fault and I was crazy for suspecting him."

Heartsick and disappointed—but also aware that relapse was part of the disease of addiction—Mary refused to be drawn into an argument. Instead, she calmly told her husband that she loved him but could no longer live with active addiction. If he chose to get help and get back into recovery, he could continue to live at home. If not, he would have to find somewhere else to live. The choice was his.

That night, he went off to a meeting as usual. When he came home, he tearfully admitted that she was right. He had relapsed, and he asked her to give him another chance. "Now, he's more committed to his recovery than ever," Mary said. "But we don't take anything for granted. It's one day at a time."

Mary was fortunate in that she had learned a lot about addiction from others who had been in her situation. She knew that she could not assume responsibility for her husband's recovery. That responsibility lay solely with him. She also knew that reacting to his relapse with anger or blame or self-pity would only make things worse. Instead, she showed love and support, asked him to get help, and clearly defined her own boundaries.

Fortunately, her husband was receptive, and he was soon back on track.

But it doesn't always work out that way.

Dealing with Relapse

Sometimes we try our best to be encouraging and supportive, but relapse happens anyway. When that happens, it is easy to become discouraged and fear that our loved one is a "lost cause." In our despair, we can succumb to fatalistic thinking and conclude that things will never get better.

It is at just such times that we need to step back and draw on our own inner sources of faith and hope. After all, our own recovery from the trauma of a loved one's addiction depends on focusing on our own well-being, no matter what is going on in the addict's life. Part of protecting our well-being includes maintaining the boundaries between ourselves and our loved one. No matter how much we want her to succeed, and no matter how much our hearts ache to watch her struggle, we cannot allow the line between our loved one and ourselves to become blurred.

A friend of mine expressed this point quite clearly one night when we were on the phone. I was lamenting my daughter's latest crisis and desperately searching for some way to solve it. "I just wish I could find a job for her," I cried. "That would give her some self-respect and maybe she could make some friends."

My friend, who had listened to similar remarks from me over many years, paused a moment. "It's hard enough trying to figure out how to live one life," she said. "It must be really hard trying to figure out how to live two."

I was taken aback, but she was right. I was trying to live my daughter's life for her, a pattern I have struggled mightily against but one that I still find myself slipping into in moments of crisis. It's a response pattern that does neither one of us any good.

During the years of active addiction, we learn that our lives become chaotic and unmanageable when we allow the addicts' struggles to become our own. It is a lesson that is no less important during their struggles in recovery. Furthermore, it is only by maintaining our perspective as separate individuals—*detachment,* in the language of Al-Anon—that we can see the situation more clearly and offer the kind of support that may be truly helpful.

By being detached, we avoid falling into the same trap of negative thinking that the relapsing addict has fallen into. Instead, we can offer some fundamental truths about relapse: (1) it is part of the recovery process; (2) a relapse is an opportunity for learning and growing; (3) the recovery that has been acquired prior to the relapse is not lost, for the addict still has important knowledge and information; and (4) our loved one has achieved sobriety at least once, and she can do so again.

As one counselor pointed out, relapses can provide a powerful lesson about the insidious nature of addiction and underscore the need for a strong recovery program. Many addicts have a lingering desire to be able to use their substance of choice and not have serious consequences. A relapse is, in a way, a testing of that fantasy. Having been clean for a while and having achieved some semblance of a normal life, they may begin to believe that their addiction wasn't as bad as they'd thought.

"When I relapsed for the third time," one woman recalled, "I'd been sober two years. I was at a wedding reception and I had one glass of wine. I told myself I was cured, I could handle it. And I did. I had one glass of wine. The next day, after the kids went to school, I bought a bottle of rum. A week later, I was in the hospital. It took almost killing myself for me to figure out once and for all that I can't drink like other people. I just can't."

When a relapse happens, it is probably natural to feel that a failure has taken place. But the lesson of relapse is not that our loved one has failed. It is that she has more lessons to learn, more growing to do. Relapse is another step in the journey, not the end of the road.

RECOVERY—OR NOT

We hope for a full, picture-perfect recovery for our loved one: He will go into treatment, achieve sobriety, and lead a healthy, responsible, fulfilling life. Wanting the people we care about to achieve the best that life has to offer is the very definition of love.

Often, the path of recovery leads to exactly that (with life's inevitable ups and downs, of course). The spiritual components of recovery, which include self-knowledge, integrity, and compassion, provide a strong foundation for a rich and rewarding life.

But sometimes the path of recovery is incomplete. Sometimes it can meander in an undirected, unfinished way, like a road that peters out without seeming to lead anywhere in particular. The addict may have reduced the use of alcohol or other drugs but continue to dabble on weekends or certain occasions. The addict may have stopped using the primary drug of choice, such as methamphetamines or heroin, but continue to drink alcohol and smoke pot. Or the addict may abstain from substances of abuse altogether but continue to have significant emotional, social, and vocational challenges. (The term *dry drunk* refers to the person who has attained sobriety but has failed to improve his psychological and social functioning.)

In these cases, when the recovery journey seems stalled, stymied, and incomplete, the result is what's sometimes called partial recovery, but might more accurately be described as modified addiction. Days are no longer devoted exclusively to the pursuit and use of substances—which indicates a change of consciousness within the addict—even though other desirable aspects of recovery have yet to be attained.

To relate incomplete recovery to the stages of change, it is as if the addict is balancing on a seesaw with precontemplation on one end and action on the other; not yet ready to acknowledge the full severity of the problem but willing to take certain steps to improve the situation. This uneasy position, which seemingly could tip either way at any moment, can create distress for both the addict and the family. The addict who has taken only tentative steps toward recovery experiences the inner turmoil we all experience when we're torn between one course of action and another. The family, aware that unhealthy behaviors are continuing, keeps hoping for the best and fearing the worst.

The Certainty of Uncertainty

My daughter seemed on the verge of recovery for many years. As a methadone maintenance patient, she gave up heroin but continued to smoke pot and drink alcohol. She went through phases of attending Twelve Step meetings on a regular basis and phases of paying no attention to recovery at all (as far as I could tell—we never really know another's inner struggles). Her sporadic attempts at going to school and holding a job were unsuccessful. She bounced from one miserable relationship to another. When I saw her two or three times a month—usually at a restaurant for breakfast or dinner—she was frequently anxious or sad.

By then, I had attended enough Al-Anon and Nar-Anon meetings to know I could not force her into recovery any more than I had been able to prevent her from being addicted. I knew that focusing on my own personal growth was paramount, both for my own well-being and my daughter's. Nevertheless, I was often in a state of low-level anxiety. I was frustrated by what I saw as her unwillingness to take charge of her own life and her indifference to my worries.

One evening, we slid into a booth at her favorite restaurant. There were tears in her eyes. "No, I don't have any good news to tell you, so don't even ask!" she declared before I had said more than *hello.* "You should just forget about me."

"Why would I want to do that? I love you."

"But you don't deserve this. Every time I see you, I wish I had something good to tell you, but I never do. You shouldn't have to worry about me anymore."

I was moved. My daughter had revealed her inner turmoil and her awareness of how her actions affected me. She was not indifferent to my worries, as I sometimes feared, and she was not willfully wasting her life. She was simply stuck.

Later on, when she had calmed down, she admitted as much. "I know what I should do," she lamented. "I don't know why I don't do it."

That, in a nutshell, is the dilemma of addicts who have taken steps to improve their condition but are unwilling to fully commit to recovery. No longer unaware of the negative effects of addiction on their lives, recognizing that some sort of change is needed, they are for some reason stuck between action and inaction. (And haven't we all been similarly stuck at some point in our lives?)

How long does this condition last? There is no way to know. Studies have shown that it may be a permanent state, a step toward recovery, or a precursor to relapse. (Relapse may be a necessary learning experience before recovery is fully embraced.) The hope is that the ongoing discomfort of the situation will eventually lead the addict to seek a positive resolution. After all, pain can be a powerful motivator for change.

I reminded my daughter of that at some point during our conversation. "Maybe the fact that you're so unhappy is a good thing," I said. "Maybe it's a sign that you're getting ready to change. Would you be willing to talk to a counselor about it?"

I had asked her the same question many times before and had been met with a marked lack of enthusiasm. To my surprise, this time she readily agreed.

Would the new counselor make a difference? Would her growing dissatisfaction with her life lead her to embrace recovery? Or would she decide that the struggle was too great and relapse to a greater level of substance abuse?

There was no way to know which way the seesaw would tip. I wanted to know the outcome. I wanted some certainty. But I had to accept the inevitable uncertainty of life. I knew that my daughter had a foundation for recovery—however shaky. I knew that the seeds of change were growing within her.

Beyond that, I had to trust that she would find her path to recovery in her own time and in her own way.

TIPS FOR DEALING WITH A SLIP OR RELAPSE

Supporting the Addict

1. Acknowledge reality. If you suspect that a slip or relapse is about to happen, don't ignore it. Give your loved one a chance to talk about it. Don't nag or pry, but let your loved one know that you've noticed some changes and you're concerned. Ignoring a potential problem will not make it go away.

2. Allow your loved one to make recovery his number one priority. He may need to spend more time at meetings and with sober friends than you would like. Allow him to develop the support he needs.

3. Avoid shame and blame. Slips and relapses trigger intense feelings of guilt in the addict. Guilt and shame are among the biggest obstacles to recovery. Remind your loved one of personal strengths and past successes. Emphasize that she has succeeded in the past and she can do it again.

4. Encourage your loved one to get help. If a slip or relapse has happened, professional help may be called for. Depending on the severity of the situation, suggest going back into treatment, attending more Twelve Step meetings, talking to a sponsor, or seeing a counselor.

5. Put a slip or relapse into perspective. Remind your loved one that slips and relapses are a normal part of the recovery process. They are not a sign of failure. They are another opportunity for growth.

Supporting Yourself

1. Be prepared for relapse. You can't live in a constant state of expecting the worst. But recognize that relapse is a possibility, and avoid getting your hopes up too high too soon.

2. Don't lose your hard-earned serenity. Keep the focus on maintaining your personal well-being. Pay attention to your physical, emotional, and spiritual health. Continue to pursue personal interests.

3. Get support. Most of us are not able to cope with a loved one's addiction without support from others. The same is true of relapse. Step up your attendance at Al-Anon or Nar-Anon meetings or other support groups. Talk to a counselor. Don't go it alone.

4. Remember the old lessons of dealing with addiction: Define your boundaries (what you will and won't accept), don't enable, and detach emotionally as much as possible.

5. Have a relapse action plan and put it into effect. Will you allow your loved one to continue to live at home? If so, under what conditions? Are you willing to provide transportation to meetings, treatment, or other sources of support? Offer support only to the extent that you can do so without enabling—and without undermining your own peace of mind.

CHAPTER 6

✢

A TIME FOR HEALING

Everything flowers, from within, of self-blessing;
though sometimes it is necessary
to reteach a thing its loveliness . . .
  —GALWAY KINNELL

"Everything was always about Adam," says Chris, a forty-one-year-old computer programmer with a wife and two children. "As a kid, I never caused any trouble. Followed the rules. Paid my own way through college. But the way my parents acted, you would've thought my sister and I didn't even exist."

Chris folds his arms over his chest and leans back in a chair in his home office. He's a tall man with thinning hair and dark brown eyes, a friend of a friend who's agreed to tell me about his experiences as an addict's brother.

"Adam's six years older than me. It's Adam, then my sister, then me," Chris continues. "I used to idolize him when I was a kid. You know how brothers are. He taught me how to throw a ball. He would make up these fantastic stories about monsters and outer space. He was a good guy."

"What happened?"

Chris hesitates. "Who knows? I guess he started drinking when he was around fifteen. And then came pot and all the rest of it. And before you know it, my mom's a total wreck, and my dad's always bailing him out, and all we ever hear is 'Adam this and Adam that.'" He shakes his head. "I remember my sister saying one time, 'What's a person gotta do? Become a drug addict to get any attention around here?'"

I state the obvious. "It's hard watching your kid destroy his life."

"I suppose." He shrugs. "They didn't seem too concerned about my life or my sister's. I mean, the guy used them over and over again. Every time he walked in the house, something went missing. He actually cleaned out their checking account. And he was still the center of their world."

I'm at a loss for words. I myself was guilty of showering attention on my addicted daughter while assuming my other two children could handle their own lives. It is only in looking back that I can see how unhealthy our family had become. "What's the situation like now?"

"Adam's been clean about two years. I guess we're all supposed to forgive and forget. One big happy family." He scratches his chin. "I don't know what it's going to take for that to happen. Some kind of miracle."

Maybe, I think. Maybe a miracle, or a lot of hard work.

THE DAMAGE DONE

Most addicts' lives are littered with the remains of damaged relationships. Many of them have manipulated, lied to, or stolen from the very people who love them most. They have failed to shoulder their share of responsibilities, and they have let down friends and family over and over again. Their hurtful behavior has caused heartache and anxiety and turmoil within the family—while they have gone about their lives with apparent disregard for the feelings of others.

Despite the worry that friends and family members are likely to feel during the early days of addiction, other emotions may begin to creep in: anger, resentment, contempt, and distrust. Even if we recognize that it is the addiction, not the person, behind the destructive behaviors, we are affected emotionally. Unhealthy patterns of relating with our loved one are likely to develop.

"No matter what the conversation was about, it always ended in an argument," said one man of the years of his wife's active drinking.

"I spent a lot of time giving him the silent treatment or crying alone in my room," recalled a woman whose husband was addicted to cocaine.

"I became a screamer," said another woman. "I guess I thought if I screamed loud enough and long enough, he'd change."

A man recalled that he simply adopted the habit of pretending that everything was all right. "It was easier to ignore my wife's addiction to prescription painkillers than to try to do anything. I closed my eyes," he said.

All of these behaviors—rejecting, scorning, fighting, and ignoring, along with a whole host of other defensive postures—are ways of protecting ourselves from experiencing more pain. When we focus our attention on lashing out or retreating into angry silence, we partially or temporarily blunt the impact of our loved one's hurtful acts.

When our loved one begins to recover from his addiction, we usually find ourselves locked in old patterns of interacting with him. He may be changing, but we cannot dismantle our emotional framework overnight. We cannot, as Chris put it, simply "forgive and forget" on a moment's notice. Furthermore, he may continue to behave in ways we find upsetting. He may "selfishly" focus most of his energy on his recovery and ignore our needs and desires. And he may be unwilling to address our grievances that have built up over the years.

These are legitimate concerns that point to the reasons why early recovery can be a relationship landmine. The combination of deep wounds (on both sides), rising expectations, and changing sensibilities makes it hard to establish the trust, respect, and honest communication that form the bedrock of all healthy relationships.

HEALING RELATIONSHIPS

Despite these very real difficulties, the early recovery of our addicted loved one is a time of great promise. Relationships can begin to heal as family members find healthier, more nurturing ways of interacting with each other. The pain of the past can begin to be replaced with understanding and hope. But making these positive changes is almost always a long, slow process.

"It doesn't happen overnight," warned one woman whose son has been clean and sober almost eight years. "But we can all get there."

A good place to begin is by taking a closer look at our assumptions and expectations.

Assessing Our Assumptions

When Maureen's father ended a twelve-month stint as the manager of a sober house and moved into his own apartment, she thought that he was getting his life back on track. He had been sober almost two years, he had a decent job, and he was doing his best to establish a loving relationship with his grandchildren. At long last, he was getting his head on straight, she thought.

"My dad was always terrible with money," she recalled. "I thought that now he was sober, he'd be more responsible. You know, save a little bit, stop wasting it on restaurants, and things like that. But he was the same as always—broke by the end of the week. I nagged him about it constantly."

Maureen believed that security came from holding on to her money. She liked having a comfortable nest egg. It made her feel safe. She assumed that deep down, her dad wanted that same financial security. She was wrong.

"It took me a long time to understand that he doesn't look at money the same way I do," she said. "He'd rather enjoy it today and worry about tomorrow tomorrow. That's just how he is."

That insight allowed her to let go of trying to manage his finances and eased much of the tension between them. More important, it opened her eyes to the pitfalls of assuming she knew more about her father than she actually did.

In general, our assumptions about others fall into two broad categories: assuming that what is important to us is important to them and assuming that we know what they are thinking and feeling. Both kinds of assumptions can get us into trouble in our relationships with others.

We have all had experiences in which our assumptions have been proven wrong. For example, we might assume that a neighbor didn't say hello because she's mad at us, when in fact she didn't even see us. We might assume that our son was irritable during dinner because he couldn't borrow the car, when what he was really thinking about was the spat he'd had with his girlfriend. We might assume that a prospective employer hasn't called us because we blew the interview, when in reality he's been called out of town.

Making assumptions during early recovery is especially problematic because it can cut the lines of communication before they're even connected.

In the unknown territory of our loved one's recovery, we have nothing to guide us other than her past behavior, which most likely has been appalling. So when she is withdrawn or irritable, we can be quick to assume that she has started using again. When she procrastinates about looking for a job or going back to school, we can tell ourselves that she's lazy or unmotivated. When she doesn't want to participate in a family activity that's important to us, we can conclude that she is selfish or rebellious.

In reality, there could be many reasons for our loved one's behaviors, including such self-defeating emotions as fear, shame, and embarrassment. She might be paralyzed by a lack of know-how or skills. She could be struggling with a problem we're entirely unaware of.

The point is, we will never find out what she is thinking or feeling unless we let go of our assumptions. Assumptions create barriers to communication because we are tuned in to what's going on inside our own head, all the while telling ourselves it's what's going on in hers.

It is only by approaching our loved one with an open mind that is free of prejudgment and false assumptions that we make it possible for honest communication to begin.

Unspoken Expectations

Unspoken expectations are another common stumbling block to rebuilding relationships. Our daily lives are filled with them: If we e-mail a friend, we'll get a response; if we do someone a favor, we'll receive a thank-you; if we invite people to our home, they'll show up on time. These kinds of expectations form a kind of social contract between people. As long as everyone has a basic agreement on the rules of the contract, the wheels of social interaction run fairly smoothly.

But problems can pop up when the people involved don't share the same set of expectations, when they aren't playing by the same rules. The truth of this hit home for me a while back when I took it upon myself to make a doctor's appointment for my daughter. She had a rash and had scheduled an appointment for herself at a local dermatologist's office. The problem was that she would have to wait a week to see him. I decided that was too long to wait and found a doctor who could see her the following day.

She didn't show up for the appointment.

I was disappointed and a little bit hurt. After all, I'd gone to a lot of trouble to find a doctor. I expected her to follow through and get treated right away. I expected her to be grateful for what I had done.

But those were my expectations, not hers. She had expected to be allowed to handle her problem on her own. By interfering where I had not been invited and then anticipating that she would respond as I had imagined, I had set myself up for disappointment.

Sorting out the role of expectations in our relationships can be confusing. A friend of mine confided, "When I have expectations, they get me in trouble. I have *hope* that I'll be all right because I've done what I need to do to take care of myself. I *trust* that no matter what happens, I'll be all right. But I made a conscious decision not to expect. It's about unlearning the things that hurt us."

How do expectations have the potential to hurt us? When we put our trust in someone who is not trustworthy, or when we fail to establish a shared set of rules of behavior, we are likely to get hurt.

One woman recalled, "During the days of my sister's active addiction, I often invited her to stop by the house on Sundays. I missed her, and that was the one day of the week I didn't work. She'd always agree to come over, but she never did. Still, I kept expecting her to keep her word. By one o'clock, my stomach would start knotting up. By two, I'd feel sick. By three, I'd be teary. And by four, I'd be totally depressed. This went on for a year or more before I finally stopped asking her. I made a point to keep myself busy on Sundays."

She paused before adding with a wry smile, "I guess I set myself up by expecting more than she was able to do at that time."

Of course, it's no surprise that expecting active addicts to keep their word is a losing proposition. What can be surprising is that it is equally fruitless to expect our loved one's social skills to have miraculously improved during early recovery.

Boundaries versus Expectations

The early months and years of recovery are often marked by continued impairment of emotional and social functioning. These symptoms generally improve over time, but it can take many years before the damaging effects of addiction are replaced by healthy behavior.

Our loved one simply hasn't had much practice in holding up his end of the social contract. He may not know—as in the case of my daughter—how to frankly state that he doesn't want our help or that he wants to be left alone. He may not know how to take care of his own needs, much less anticipate ours. (Of course, all of this can be true for nonaddicts, as well.)

One of the most effective things we can do to help our loved one strengthen relationship skills is to openly discuss expectations—ours and hers. Far too often, we don't clearly express what we want or need. We expect our loved ones to be mind readers and are disappointed when they don't respond as we had hoped. The woman who fumes silently while her family goes off to watch television and leaves her with a kitchen full of dirty dishes and the man who grits his teeth and says nothing when his son repeatedly brings the car home with the gas tank near empty have both failed to make their expectations clear.

It's true that clarifying expectations does not guarantee that family members will pitch in with the dishes or put gas in the car. But having a discussion about expectations at least opens the door to negotiation and creates an environment where positive change can happen.

My friend who claims to have given up expectations said that she has replaced them with a clear set of boundaries. She put them into practice one Christmas Eve when she hosted her traditional family gathering in her home. Her son had recently relapsed and, to top it off, had had an affair with his wife's best friend.

"I made a decision to have everyone over as usual—my kids, grandkids, nephews, his estranged wife—everyone. But I told everyone as they arrived that I wasn't going to permit one negative thing. The kids deserved a good Christmas and we were going to give it to them. And every time someone started to say something negative, I said no. There was no pretending that something hadn't happened. It just wasn't the focus that evening. And we had fun. We played games, laughed. It was beautiful."

She explained, "I had made that decision. I made the rules. And once that was clear, everyone knew what the rules were and we could just relax."

By setting the rules and explicitly stating her boundaries— instead of leaving people to guess about her unspoken expectations—she made it easier for her family to enjoy their time together and have a positive experience.

THE ROLES WE PLAY

The term *dysfunctional family* has become something of a cliché. Some people claim that most families are dysfunctional in one way or another. There's an element of truth in this. After all, we humans are full of contradictions and character flaws, and when we are put together in a close unit—such as a family—all types of unhealthy behaviors and dynamics are bound to develop.

But a dysfunctional family is not simply a collection of people who don't get along sometimes. It is one in which the growth of its individual members is sacrificed to the perceived greater good and security of the family unit. Family members are handicapped in their journey toward growth by the roles they assume to keep the family system going as it is, to preserve it from falling apart or changing.

Most families impacted by addiction will become at least somewhat dysfunctional. As the addict consumes more and more of the family's attention and energy, unhealthy behavioral patterns are likely to emerge, including denial, dishonesty, obsession, enabling, manipulation, self-pity, and anger. Family members will unknowingly take on roles that embody those behaviors and minimize or distract the family from its root problems.

The "caretaker," for example, will be the problem-solver who fixes everything, and in the process probably does a lot of enabling. The "hero" will be the overachiever who strives to be perfect and maintain the family's good image. The "lost child" will try to reduce the family's stress by having no individual needs and causing no problems. The "clown" will act the playful fool to make the situation seem less dire. And the "scapegoat"—the addict—will become the sole source and repository of the family's problems and unhappiness.

These roles, which emerge in response to family distress, are extremely damaging to each individual's sense of identity. Family members can become defined by the parts they play, confined in narrow bands of learned behaviors that limit their ability to grow socially and emotionally. Furthermore, their sense of themselves as being a particular kind of person is often reinforced by other family members. My daughter, for example, used to refer to herself as "the black sheep" (a variation of the scapegoat), an indication that she saw herself as someone who always got into trouble or messed things up. It didn't help that her siblings and I often saw her precisely that way.

Roles limit our vision of self and others. When we view the world through a narrow lens, we tend to confirm what we expect to see and miss out on the bigger picture of what exists or what is possible. This can complicate matters when an addicted loved one—the scapegoat—begins to recover.

For example, we may habitually see our addicted loved one as fundamentally helpless and ourselves as someone who must take control (an unhealthy dynamic that developed between my daughter and me). By projecting a negative image onto the addict and claiming a position of power for ourselves, we create tension within the relationship. The addict is likely to resent being treated like a child, and we are likely to resent when things don't go as planned.

The solution is to learn to let go of our long-held perceptions. In reality, our loved one is not helpless, and we are not obliged—

or for that matter, able—to manage her life for her. The roles that have defined us both, perhaps for a very long time, are no longer valid as recovery progresses.

One of the most significant challenges facing addicts in early recovery is redefining themselves. We, too, as family members who have adopted unhealthy roles in response to addiction, face the challenge of creating new ways of seeing ourselves, both within the family system and as individuals. Our relationships can begin to heal only if we are willing to examine familiar patterns of interacting and become open to new ways of seeing our loved ones and ourselves.

The Drama Triangle

In the 1960s, Stephen Karpman introduced a way of looking at the roles we play. He created a behavioral model called the Drama Triangle, which consists of three roles: the persecutor, the victim, and the rescuer. Interestingly, it requires only two actors. Each person constantly changes roles as the scene unfolds.

To get an idea of how it works, consider the following scenario in which Bob's wife, Jean, comes home from an AA meeting half an hour later than she had promised:

Bob (victim):	You said you'd be home by nine. I was worried sick.
Jean (rescuer):	I'm sorry. I know I should have called. I don't mean to make you worry.
Bob (persecutor):	Well, you do it all the time. You never think of anyone but yourself.
Jean (victim):	That's not true. I just got talking to some people and I lost track of the time. I'm sorry I'm not perfect. I always let you down.
Bob (rescuer):	Not always. I know you try. And you've

	been doing a lot better. I just wish you would have called.
Jean (persecutor):	You put so much pressure on me. Sometimes I don't know if you want to be my husband or my father.
Bob (victim):	I guess it's wrong for me to care. Maybe you'd be happier if I didn't worry about you at all.
Jean (rescuer):	Of course I want you to care.
Bob (persecutor):	It would be nice if you'd learn to show it.
Jean (victim):	And it would be nice if you'd learn to show a little trust . . .

The conversation could go on like this for hours, with both people feeling wronged and nothing getting resolved. In the meantime, the real issues that need to be negotiated—how Bob can better handle his anxiety when his wife is late and how she can be more considerate of his concerns—get swept aside in the drama of the moment.

Interactions like this happen all too frequently in our daily lives. We get caught up in emotions, and instead of trying to find a solution to a problem, we compete to cast ourselves as the injured party—for it is the victim who plays the starring role in the Drama Triangle. When the victim bows out, the drama collapses.

A psychologist I once consulted said that one of the surest routes to emotional health is to let go of the idea that any adult is actually a victim in a relationship. "Sometimes people hurt us or let us down. That doesn't make us a victim. That's part of life," he said. "Being a victim means being helpless, not having a choice. But we all have choices in how we respond to other people, where we focus our attention, what we do with our emotions. Playing the victim keeps relationships stuck and prevents us from moving forward."

When we are the victim, we are not responsible for our choices or our actions. Someone else is to blame, and someone else has the responsibility for making things better.

In our dealings with our addicted loved one, we have no doubt had many opportunities to feel like a victim. Even when our loved one is in recovery, we can feel taken advantage of or neglected—in short, victimized—when he fails to meet our needs. (Conversely, we may be inclined to cast our loved one as victim—something I was prone to do with my daughter.)

But being a victim simply perpetuates the Drama Triangle and distracts us from our responsibility to focus on our own lives. When we let go of seeing ourselves or our loved one as a victim, we can close the curtain on the Drama Triangle and set the stage for personal growth and healthier relationships.

THE FINE ART OF LISTENING

When Sarah's grown son confessed that he had lost his third job in less than a year, she rushed to his defense. "I'm going to call your boss and tell him what I think of him," she declared. "Your problem is you don't know how to stick up for yourself."

Sarah's frustration was understandable. Her son, who had a history of addiction as well as a criminal record, had been clean and sober for almost two years. He was doing his best to get his life on track, but it seemed that every time an employer found out about his past, her son got the boot. Sarah was determined to be there for him.

Her heated response to his perceived (and perhaps real) unfair treatment did nothing to promote her son's growth in recovery and nothing to nurture their fragile relationship. In her effort to be supportive, she had neglected to use one of the most effective tools for helping others and strengthening relationships: listening.

On the face of it, listening seems like a pretty easy thing to do. It's a normal part of human interaction, something we do every day. But effective listening goes beyond hearing the spoken word.

It is a communication style that builds connections by demonstrating understanding, empathy, and encouragement.

Too often, our conversations with loved ones build walls instead of bridges. One way we do this is by bringing our own preconceived ideas to the table. For example, Sarah's perception of her son was that he was too laid-back, too willing to let people walk all over him. Instead of giving him the opportunity to talk about what was going on, she jumped to the conclusion that she knew what the problem was.

Sarah undoubtedly hoped that her show of concern would make her son feel better, but she probably diminished his self-confidence by implying that he was not capable of fighting his own battles and that his own personality was the reason he kept losing his jobs. Because he felt worse about himself after talking with her, he might be less willing to share his problems with her in the future.

In addition to the damaging impact of preconceived ideas, our listening skills falter when we feel responsible for solving our loved one's problems. Often, the simple act of talking about things that are troubling us can lighten our emotional burden. In hearing our own spoken words, we sometimes discover new insights into our situation and work out solutions that weren't apparent before. But the benefit of talking is short-circuited when the person on the listening end jumps in with ways to "fix" the problem. Our thought processes are interrupted and we begin to question our own instincts.

I know a woman whose daughter jokingly tells her friends, "Don't ask my mother for advice because she'll just say you'll figure it out." Her mother happens to be someone many people turn to when they need a sympathetic ear. Her great gift is that she listens carefully, doesn't offer advice, and sincerely believes in others' ability to resolve their own problems.

"My daughter is really struggling right now," she recently told me.

"She's been clean seven years, and the other day she called and said she's afraid she might pick up after all these years. She's in a very dark place. I reminded her that recovery teaches us we have to walk through our pain and not run away from it. We have to take a good look at it and feel it. And that made sense to her. But I also know that I can't interfere. All I can do is tell her that I love her, that I'm here for her, and that she knows what she has to do. She knows."

When we offer our loved one that kind of listening—acknowledging the reality of the situation without having to fix it—we help our relationships heal. Our loved one learns that it's safe to tell us things without being judged or jeopardizing control of her own life. And, through our willingness to listen with an open mind and heart, we begin to understand her on a deeper level.

REBUILDING TRUST

When addicts begin to recover, trust is one of the first things they long for, but it may be one of the last things they are able to reestablish in their lives. The wounds they have caused are generally too deep and the disappointments too numerous for trust to come easily to the people who love them.

It is common for addicts in early recovery to complain that they've been clean six months, twelve months, two years, and their families still don't trust them. But with growth in recovery, most of them come to recognize that loss of trust is an inevitable consequence of addiction.

One woman recalled telling her children that she was about to receive her first-year sobriety coin in AA, only to hear, "Congratulations. Let us know when you get your coin next year." They told her the same thing when she got her second-year coin. It wasn't until a year later that her children were finally willing to attend the meeting with her. Her son and daughter presented their mother her three-year coin. "It took that long for them to believe that I was finally serious about recovery," she said. "It took that long to regain their trust."

Another woman said, "My dad used to always watch me. He was always suspicious. It made me mad, but I couldn't really blame him."

Hope, who raised her grandchildren during her daughter's long addiction, said that trust returns slowly during recovery, but questions always remain. "My daughter has been clean eight years. She's become an incredible woman," she said. "But I still ask myself sometimes, *Is she going to use again? Is she going to steal again?* Is there ever a point when you stop worrying about that? Yes. But I don't think there'll ever be a time when a thought from the past might not come back."

It's what we do with those thoughts, she believes, that shows where we are in our own recovery. "When your addict is using, you would never leave anything of value around," she explained. "You know what's going to happen and you'd be foolish to do so. Now I don't put my pocketbook away when my daughter's in the house. But the thought's there. It comes into my brain. I might want to remove my pocketbook because of the past, but that's where my recovery comes in. She's not that person anymore, and neither am I. It's a deliberate decision on my part to let the past go and give each day the dignity of the present."

Ray, a recovering addict, understands firsthand the long process of rebuilding trust. "My father came to the point where he wouldn't let me in the house," he said. "One time, I went to his place of employment and asked to borrow three dollars. He said he wouldn't give me money to buy that shit and threw me out. Three years after I was clean, I asked him to cosign for a motorcycle. He loaned me fifteen thousand dollars. He gave me land to build a house. My parents chose to make me their medical proxy. That's the kind of faith they have, the kind of trust. Because I'm responsible, I'm a man of my word today."

He paused and added, "Eight short years ago, I was bumming quarters at Dunkin' Donuts. It's incredible to me—eight short years."

The lesson that Ray and other recovering addicts have come to accept is that trust has to be earned. We, as family members, have the right to determine how quickly and to what extent we are willing to extend our trust. After all, trust makes us vulnerable to hurt and disappointment. It makes sense to keep our guard up, at least for a while.

But it also makes sense to remember that it is only by allowing ourselves to trust again, when the time is right, that our relationships have the potential to fully heal.

THE JOURNEY OF A LIFETIME

For many of us whose loved one is still in the earliest stages of recovery, the potential for a healed, healthy relationship remains just that—a potential. Our loved one may still be too fragile to begin to repair his relationships. His need for space may still be greater than his need for family connections. And we may as yet be unwilling or unable to extend our trust and forgiveness.

That is okay. One of the cardinal, inalterable rules of recovery is that it can't be rushed. It takes as long as it takes. Still, it is worth remembering that every day is a new day, and that the future can be infinitely brighter than the past.

For Ray, recovery has brought rewards beyond anything he could have imagined during his twenty-five years of addiction. "My war cry for many, many years was, 'Stay out of my business. I'm not hurting anybody but myself,'" he said. "But hindsight is twenty-twenty. Looking back on anybody who cared anything about me, I can see I caused a great deal of pain. I was truly incapable of knowing what true love, what unconditional love was. I couldn't comprehend what my family felt for me. Today I do."

Hope, who became alienated from her daughter during the years of addiction, said, "Today I have a marvelous relationship with my daughter. We share a lot. She has become an inspiration because of the things she's overcome—without my help. She had to do urine tests for six years to keep her job. It was an inconvenience, but she said, 'This is the wreckage of my past, and I'm going to do what I have to do to set things right.' She's become this woman of grace and dignity."

Sandra, whose husband's cocaine addiction almost cost them the family home and business, said, "We spent a lot of our marriage fighting. We don't do that anymore. He's learned to live with the fact that I don't share some of his interests, and when he gets in one of his difficult moods, I can ignore it. I don't have to be right anymore."

Does there ever come a time when our relationship with our recovering loved one becomes perfect? Of course not. All relationships exist in an ebb and flow of good times and bad, of certainty and doubt, of closeness and pulling away. Incidents from the past may come up for years to come, creating tension and discomfort. Long-buried resentments may rear their head in unexpected ways. Fears may creep in from time to time, threatening our hard-earned peace of mind.

Still, we can draw comfort from understanding that recovery is a journey of a lifetime. Although its challenges are tremendous, its rewards are truly life-altering.

As we begin this journey with our recovering loved one—moving toward greater understanding, compassion, and personal growth—we are fortunate indeed to be guided by those who have walked this path before us, and to be sustained by the resilient, enduring bond of family.

TIPS FOR HEALING FAMILY RELATIONSHIPS

Supporting the Addict

1. Don't assume you know more than you actually do. Your loved one may not share your opinions and perceptions. Take the time to find out how he actually feels about things.

2. Don't set your loved one up to disappoint you by harboring unrealistic expectations. Addiction has done emotional damage, and it may take a long time before she is able to give your relationship the attention it deserves.

3. Examine family roles and allow them to change. In recovery, family members can be freed from unhealthy perceptions of themselves and each other. Letting go of old roles allows everyone to become their best self.

4. Listen with love. Let go of your preconceived ideas and your sense of responsibility to fix things. Listen, instead, with an attitude of compassion, acceptance, and respect.

5. Promote hope. Hope is contagious. When you bring an attitude of hope to your relationships, you give your loved one a precious gift that will help sustain him through the long struggle to make things better.

Supporting Yourself

1. Consider family therapy. Families wounded by addiction have almost certainly developed unhealthy ways of relating to each other. Sometimes professional help is needed to bring clarity to the situation.

2. Get out of the Drama Triangle. Addiction has brought great pain to your life. But there is no room for victims in recovery. Learn, instead, to take good care of yourself no matter where your loved one is in her recovery.

3. Let go of feeling responsible for your loved one's recovery. Treating people with respect means that you don't assume they need help managing their lives. Treating yourself with respect means that you focus on your own well-being.

4. Turn the page on the past. This will not come easily. Pain and repeated disappointments have changed the way you see your addicted loved one. Trust has been broken. Still, a new chapter in your life is unfolding. This does not mean that the past can be forgotten— only that it can be put in its proper place.

5. Love yourself. Your loved one's addiction has hurt and challenged you beyond what many people could ever imagine. Yet you have survived, and even grown. Celebrate your enduring strength, and cherish your lifelong journey of personal growth.

WORDS OF INSPIRATION AND SUPPORT

Listen to the Exhortation of the Dawn!
Look to this Day!
For it is Life, the very Life of Life.
In its brief course lie all the
Verities and Realities of your Existence.
The Bliss of Growth,
The Glory of Action,
The Splendor of Beauty;
For Yesterday is but a Dream,
And Tomorrow is only a Vision;
But Today well lived makes
Every Yesterday a Dream of Happiness,
And every Tomorrow a Vision of Hope.
Look well therefore to this Day!
Such is the Salutation of the Dawn!
—KALIDASA

A major characteristic of genuine love is that the distinction between oneself
and the other is always maintained and preserved.
—M. SCOTT PECK

Attachment is the great fabricator of illusions; reality can be attained only by someone who is detached.

— SIMONE WEIL

We don't see things as they are; we see them as we are.

—ANAÏS NIN

The beginning of love is to let those we love be perfectly themselves, and not to twist them to fit our own image. Otherwise we love only the reflection of ourselves we find in them.

—THOMAS MERTON

Where love rules, there is no will to power; and where power predominates, there love is lacking. The one is the shadow of the other.

—CARL JUNG

Amazing grace! How sweet the sound
That saved a wretch like me!
I once was lost, but now am found,
Was blind, but now I see.

—JOHN NEWTON

Have courage for the great sorrows of life and patience for the small ones; and when you have laboriously accomplished your daily task, go to sleep in peace. God is awake.

—VICTOR HUGO

I think we all have a little voice inside us that will guide us. It may be God, I don't know. But I think that if we shut out all the noise and clutter from our lives and listen to that voice, it will tell us the right thing to do.

—CHRISTOPHER REEVE

*We are not born all at once, but by bits. The body first, and the spirit later;
and the birth and growth of the spirit, in those who are attentive to their
own inner life, are slow and exceedingly painful. Our mothers are racked
with the pains of our physical birth; we ourselves suffer the longer pains of
our spiritual growth.*

—MARY ANTIN

*And as we let our own light shine, we unconsciously give other people
permission to do the same. As we are liberated from our fear,
our presence automatically liberates others.*

—MARIANNE WILLIAMSON

*The truth is that our finest moments are most likely to occur when we are
feeling deeply uncomfortable, unhappy, or unfulfilled. For it is only in such
moments, propelled by our discomfort, that we are likely to step out of our
ruts and start searching for different ways or truer answers.*

—M. SCOTT PECK

*Fear imprisons, faith liberates; fear paralyzes, faith empowers;
fear disheartens, faith encourages; fear sickens, faith heals;
fear makes useless, faith makes serviceable.*

—HARRY EMERSON FOSDICK

*There are as many nights as days, and the one is just as long as the other in the
year's course. Even a happy life cannot be without a measure of darkness, and
the word 'happy' would lose its meaning if it were not balanced by sadness.*

—CARL JUNG

*It's not that some people have willpower and some don't.
It's that some people are ready to change and others are not.*

—JAMES GORDON, M.D.

Though no one can go back and make a brand new start,
anyone can start from now and make a brand new ending.
——CARL BARD

You gain strength, courage, and confidence by every experience in which you
really stop to look fear in the face. You are able to say to yourself, 'I have
lived through this horror. I can take the next thing that comes along.'
You must do the thing you think you cannot do.
——ELEANOR ROOSEVELT

Perhaps the earth can teach us
As when everything seems dead
And later proves to be alive.
——PABLO NERUDA

Don't judge each day by the harvest you reap, but by the seeds you plant.
——ROBERT LOUIS STEVENSON

We plant the seeds of love, knowing that nature will take its course and in
time those seeds will bear fruit. Some seeds will come to fruition quickly,
some slowly, but our work is simply to plant the seeds.
——SHARON SALZBURG

How poor are they who have not patience! What wound
did ever heal but by degrees.
——WILLIAM SHAKESPEARE

If you are distressed by anything external, the pain is not due to the thing
itself, but to your estimate of it; and this you have the power
to revoke at any moment.
—Marcus Aurelius

The greatest discovery of our generation is that human beings can alter their
lives by altering their attitudes of mind. As you think, so shall you be.
—William James

Everything can be taken from a man but one thing: the last of the human
freedoms—to choose one's attitude in any given set of circumstances, to
choose one's own way.
—Viktor Frankl

The difference between misery and happiness depends
on what we do with our attention.
—Sharon Salzburg

Nothing worth doing is completed in our lifetime,
Therefore, we are saved by hope.
Nothing true or beautiful or good makes complete sense in any immediate
context of history;
Therefore, we are saved by faith.
Nothing we do, however virtuous, can be accomplished alone.
Therefore, we are saved by love.
No virtuous act is quite as virtuous from the standpoint of our friend or foe
as from our own;
Therefore, we are saved by the final form of love which is forgiveness.
—Reinhold Niebuhr

Love is patient and kind; love does not envy or boast; it is not arrogant or rude. It does not insist on its own way; it is not irritable or resentful; it does not rejoice at wrongdoing, but rejoices with the truth. Love bears all things, believes all things, hopes all things, endures all things.

—1 Corinthians 13

The most basic and powerful way to connect to another person is to listen. Just listen. Perhaps the most important thing we ever give each other is our attention. . . . A loving silence often has far more power to heal and to connect than the most well-intentioned words.

—Rachel Naomi Remen

The ideals which have lighted my way, and time after time have given me new courage to face life cheerfully, have been Kindness, Beauty, and Truth. The trite subjects of human efforts—possessions, outward success, luxury— have always seemed to me contemptible.

—Albert Einstein

At times our own light goes out and is rekindled by a spark from another person. Each of us has cause to think with deep gratitude of those who have lighted the flame within us.

—Albert Schweitzer

Seeing the goodness in someone does not imply ignoring their difficult qualities. . . . Rather, we can fully acknowledge these difficulties, while at the same time we choose to focus on the positive. If we focus on the negative, we will naturally feel anger, resentment, or disappointment. If we focus on the positive, we will forge a connection to the person.

—Sharon Salzburg

Treat a man as he is, he will remain so. Treat a man the way he can be and
ought to be, and he will become as he can be and should be.
—Goethe

The world is round and the place which may seem like the end
may also be the beginning.
—Ivy Baker Priest

If you have made mistakes, even serious ones, there is always another chance
for you. What we call failure is not the falling down but the staying down.
—Mary Pickford

Freedom is not worth having if it does not include
the freedom to make mistakes.
—Mahatma Gandhi

In the event of an oxygen shortage on airplanes, mothers of young children
are always reminded to put on their own oxygen mask first, to better assist
the children with theirs. The same tactic is necessary on terra firma. There's
no way of sustaining our children if we don't first rescue ourselves. I don't
call that selfish behavior. I call it love.
—Joyce Maynard

If you would convince a man that he does wrong, do right.
Men will believe what they see.
—Henry David Thoreau

If there is anything that we wish to change in the child,
we should first examine it and see whether it is not something
that could better be changed in ourselves.
—CARL JUNG

You must be the change you want to see in the world.
—MAHATMA GANDHI

Lord, make me an instrument of Thy peace;
where there is hatred, let me sow love;
where there is injury, pardon;
where there is doubt, faith;
where there is despair, hope;
where there is darkness, light;
and where there is sadness, joy.
O Divine Master,
grant that I may not so much seek to be consoled as to console;
to be understood, as to understand;
to be loved, as to love;
for it is in giving that we receive,
it is in pardoning that we are pardoned,
and it is in dying that we are born to eternal life.
—ST. FRANCIS OF ASSISI

RESOURCES

Local chapters of Alcoholics Anonymous, Narcotics Anonymous, Al-Anon, and Nar-Anon can be found in most communities. They are all good sources of information and support. Additionally, private and public agencies that treat substance abuse usually offer educational materials and programs for families. For more information, contact any of the following organizations:

Al-Anon Family Group Headquarters, Inc.
1600 Corporate Landing Pkwy.
Virginia Beach, VA 23454-5617
757-563-1600; 888-4AL-ANON (meeting information)
www.al-anon.alateen.org

Alcoholics Anonymous World Services, Inc.
PO Box 459
New York, NY 10163
212-870-3400
www.aa.org

Center for Substance Abuse Treatment (CSAT)
Substance Abuse and Mental Health Services Administration
(SAMSHA)
1 Choke Cherry Rd.
CSAT 5th Floor
Rockville, MD 20857
204-276-2750; 800-662-HELP (treatment and support group
    referral)
www.csat.samhsa.gov

Families Anonymous, Inc.
PO Box 3475
Culver City, CA 90231-3475
800-736-9805
www.familiesanonymous.org

Hazelden
15245 Pleasant Valley Rd.
PO Box 11
Center City, MN 55012-0011
800-257-7810
www.hazelden.org

Join Together
715 Albany St., 580-3rd Floor
Boston, MA 02118
617-437-1500
www.jointogether.org

Nar-Anon Family Group Headquarters, Inc.
22527 Crenshaw Blvd. #200B
Torrance, CA 90505
310-534-8188; 800-477-6291
www.nar-anon.org

Narcotics Anonymous World Services, Inc.
PO Box 9999
Van Nuys, CA 91409
818-773-9999
www.na.org

National Clearinghouse for Alcohol and Drug Information
(NCADI)
PO Box 2345
Rockville, MD 20847-2345
800-729-6686; 240-221-4019
www.health.org

National Council on Alcoholism and Drug Dependence, Inc.
(NCADD)
244 E. 58th St., 4th Floor
New York, NY 10022
212-269-7797; 800-NCA-CALL (twenty-four-hour referral line)
www.ncadd.org

National Families in Action (NFIA)
2957 Clairmont Rd. NE, Ste. 150
Atlanta, GA 30329
404-248-9676
www.nationalfamilies.org

National Federation of Families for Children's Mental Health
9605 Medical Center Dr., Ste. 280
Rockville, MD 20850
240-403-1901
www.ffcmh.org

National Institute on Drug Abuse (NIDA)
National Institutes of Health
6001 Executive Blvd., Rm. 5213
Bethesda, MD 20892-9561
301-443-1124
www.nida.nih.gov

Recovery Month
Substance Abuse and Mental Health Services Administration
(SAMSHA)
1 Choke Cherry Rd.
CSAT 5th Floor
Rockville, MD 20857
204-276-2750
www.recoverymonth.gov

Recommended Readings

For further reading on the process of recovery from addiction, the following materials may be helpful:

Beattie, Melody. *Codependent No More: How to Stop Controlling Others and Start Caring for Yourself.* Center City, Minn.: Hazelden, 1987.

Black, Claudia. *It Will Never Happen to Me: Growing Up with Addiction as Youngsters, Adolescents, Adults.* 2nd ed. Center City, Minn.: Hazelden, 2001.

Conyers, Beverly. *Addict in the Family: Stories of Loss, Hope, and Recovery.* Center City, Minn.: Hazelden, 2003.

DuPont, Robert L. *The Selfish Brain: Learning from Addiction.* Center City, Minn.: Hazelden, 1997.

Jay, Jeff, and Jerry Boriskin. *At Wit's End: What Your Need to Know When a Loved One Is Diagnosed with Addiction and a Mental Illness.* Center City, Minn.: Hazelden, 2007.

Kettelhack, Guy. *First-Year Sobriety: When All That Changes Is Everything.* Center City, Minn.: Hazelden, 1992.

Ortman, Dennis. *The Dual Diagnosis Recovery Sourcebook: A Physical, Mental, and Spiritual Approach to Addiction with an Emotional Disorder.* Chicago: Contemporary Books, 2001.

Sheff, David. *Beautiful Boy: A Father's Journey through his Son's Addiction.* Boston: Houghton Mifflin Company, 2008.

Sheff, Nic. *Tweak: Growing Up on Methamphetamines.* New York: Simon & Schuster, 2007.

Small, Jacquelyn. *Becoming Naturally Therapeutic: A Return to the True Essence of Helping.* New York: Bantam Books, 1990.

Today's Gift: Daily Meditations for Families. Center City, Minn.: Hazelden, 1985.

Twerski, Abraham. *Addictive Thinking: Understanding Self-Deception.* Center City, Minn.: Hazelden, 1997.

THE TWELVE STEPS OF AL-ANON

1. We admitted we were powerless over alcohol—that our lives had become unmanageable.
2. Came to believe that a Power greater than ourselves could restore us to sanity.
3. Made a decision to turn our will and our lives over to the care of God *as we understood Him.*
4. Made a searching and fearless moral inventory of ourselves.
5. Admitted to God, to ourselves, and to another human being the exact nature of our wrongs.
6. Were entirely ready to have God remove all these defects of character.
7. Humbly asked Him to remove our shortcomings.
8. Made a list of all persons we had harmed, and became willing to make amends to them all.
9. Made direct amends to such people wherever possible, except when to do so would injure them or others.
10. Continued to take personal inventory and when we were wrong promptly admitted it.
11. Sought through prayer and meditation to improve our conscious contact with God *as we understood Him,* praying only for knowledge of His will for us and the power to carry that out.

12. Having had a spiritual awakening as the result of these Steps, we tried to carry this message to others, and to practice these principles in all our affairs.

The Twelve Steps of Al-Anon are taken from *Al-Anon Faces Alcoholism,* 2nd ed., published by Al-Anon Family Group Headquarters, Inc., New York, NY, 236–37.

NOTES

1. National Institute on Drug Abuse, *Principles of Drug Addiction Treatment: A Research-Based Guide,* NIH Publication No. 00-4180 (July 2000), 9–10. Can be accessed online at www.nida.nih.gov/ PODAT/PODATIndex.html.

2. New York State Office of Alcoholism and Substance Abuse Services, *Insomnia and Alcohol and Substance Abuse,* www.oasas.state .ny.us/AdMed/FYI/FYIInDepth-Insomnia.cfm.

3. Sheff, Nic, *Tweak: Growing Up on Methamphetamines* (New York: Simon & Schuster, 2007), 80.

4. Sheff, *Tweak,* 125.

5. *Blamed and Ashamed: The Treatment Experiences of Youth with Co-occurring Substance Abuse and Mental Health Disorders and Their Families* (Alexandria, Va.: Federation of Families for Children's Mental Health, 2001), 40.

6. *Blamed and Ashamed,* 44.

About the Author

Beverly Conyers is the author of *Addict in the Family: Stories of Loss, Hope, and Recovery.* She has worked as a teacher and freelance writer for many years. She lives with her family in Massachusetts and continues to be active in Twelve Step recovery programs.

Hazelden, a national nonprofit organization founded in 1949, helps people reclaim their lives from the disease of addiction. Built on decades of knowledge and experience, Hazelden offers a comprehensive approach to addiction that addresses the full range of patient, family, and professional needs, including treatment and continuing care for youth and adults, research, higher learning, public education and advocacy, and publishing.

A life of recovery is lived "one day at a time." Hazelden publications, both educational and inspirational, support and strengthen lifelong recovery. In 1954, Hazelden published *Twenty-Four Hours a Day,* the first daily meditation book for recovering alcoholics, and Hazelden continues to publish works to inspire and guide individuals in treatment and recovery, and their loved ones. Professionals who work to prevent and treat addiction also turn to Hazelden for evidence-based curricula, informational materials, and videos for use in schools, treatment programs, and correctional programs.

Through published works, Hazelden extends the reach of hope, encouragement, help, and support to individuals, families, and communities affected by addiction and related issues.

For questions about Hazelden publications,
please call **800-328-9000**
or visit us online at **hazelden.org/bookstore**.